(Not Just)

OPENERS

An Activity for Every Day of the Year!

1	2	3	4	5	6	7
8	9	10	11	12	13	14
	17	18	19	20	21	
	25	26				

Written by Rebecca Stark
Cover Illustrated by Koryn Agnello
Text Illustrated by Karen Sigler, Koryn Agnello, James Uttel and Tara Campbell

ISBN 1-56644-046-7

© 1999 Educational Impressions, Inc., Hawthorne, NJ

EDUCATIONAL IMPRESSIONS, INC.
Hawthorne, NJ 07507

Printed in the United States of America.

To the Teacher

(Not Just) Openers provides an activity for every day of the year! Use them at the beginning or end of class, as homework or enrichment assignments, or any time you choose. They may be reproduced, reduced, enlarged, and/or laminated to suit your needs. Answers and background information are provided following the activities.

These activities were originally developed for the From the First Day to the Last Series, a set of nine reproducible monthly activity books. (May and June are combined into one volume, which also contains activities for the summer months.) If you enjoy using *(Not Just) Openers*, you might also want to examine the books in that series. In addition to the (Not Just) Openers section, each volume in the series contains a wealth of interdisciplinary projects, mini-units, puzzles, clip art, and other enrichment activiites that tie in with the events and holidays of the month. Each book also includes at least one literature unit that relates in some way to the month.

Rebecca Stark

September 1

On September 1, 1865, Abraham Lincoln proposed the thirteenth amendment to the Constitution.

Find out the provisions of the thirteenth amendment.

September 2

Eugene Field was born September 2, 1850. He is known as the "Poet of Childhood."

Find out why.
Prepare an illustrated version of his most famous poem for a younger child.

September 3

Louis Sullivan was born in Boston, Massachusetts, on September 3, 1856.

Draw a picture that illustrates his accomplishments.

September 4

George Eastman received a patent on this day in 1888.

Write a letter to Mr. Eastman congratulating him for his invention and predicting its future importance.

4

September 5

The First Continental Congress met at Independence Hall in Philadelphia. Only one of the thirteen original colonies did not send representatives.

Draw a map of the thirteen colonies; show which one did not send representatives.

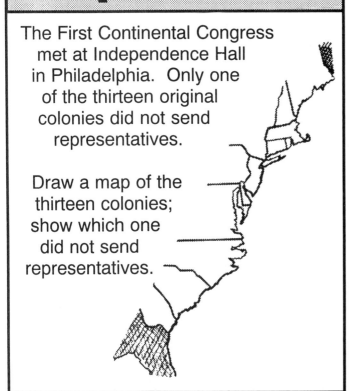

September 6

On September 6, 1901, President William McKinley was assassinated.

Find out where he was and why. Write his obituary.

September 7

Anna Mary Robertson, better known as Grandma Moses, was born on September 7, 1860. She lived to be 101.

Write three questions you might have asked her on her 100th birthday. As Grandma Moses, answer those questions.

September 8

September 8th is International Literacy Day.

Create a poster to promote literacy in your hometown.

5

September 9

On September 9, 1965, Sandy Koufax pitched a perfect game for the L.A. Dodgers. No one reached first base.

Write a letter of congratulations.

September 10

On September 10, 1813, Oliver H. Perry defeated the British at the Battle of Lake Erie.

Explain the importance of this victory to the United States.

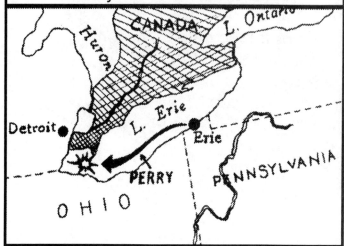

September 11

William Sidney Porter is better known by his pen name, O. Henry. He was born on September 11, 1862. His stories are known for their surprise endings.

Create the plot for a story with a surprise ending. Write a summary of the plot.

September 12

On September 12, 1940, four boys searching for a dog made a remarkable discovery in the caves of Lascaux, France.

Describe their find.

6

September 13

Milton Hershey was born on September 13, 1857. He spent years trying to perfect the chocolate bar! In 1903 he began building the world's largest chocolate manufacturing plant.

Create a poem about chocolate. Use any format you wish. Some ideas are haiku, shape poem, and acrostic.

September 14

William H. Armstrong, the author of *Sounder,* was born in Lexington, Virginia. *Sounder* tells the story of a sharecropper's family.

Write a paragraph explaining the term "sharecropper."

September 15

William Taft, the 27th President of the United States, was born on September 15, 1857. It was during his administration that the sixteenth amendment was passed.

Create a political cartoon using this amendment as the subject.

September 16

On this date in 1620 the Pilgrims left England on the *Mayflower.*

As a Pilgrim on that journey, write an entry in your diary.

September 17

On September 17, 1730, Frederich von Steuben was born.

As General George Washington, write a letter to Baron von Steuben thanking him for his assistance to the American cause. Be specific.

September 18

Renowned African-American educator Booker T. Washington addressed the Atlanta Exposition on this date in 1895.

Write an encyclopedia entry for Booker T. Washington.

September 19

On September 19, 1928, Mickey Mouse appeared for the first time in a black-and-white cartoon called *Steamboat Willie*.

See if you can find out what was special about that cartoon. Prepare three questions to ask Mickey Mouse about his debut.

September 20

Fiorello La Guardia, colorful mayor of New York City, died on September 20, 1947.

Research his life and write a eulogy for him.

8

September 21

French-Canadian fur trader, explorer, and cartographer Louis Joliet was born on September 21, 1845. Draw a map that shows the area he and Father Jacques Marquette explored.

September 22

On September 22, 1961, the Peace Corps was established.

Create a recruitment poster to encourage people to join.

September 23

On September 23, 1779, Scottish-born naval hero John Paul Jones captured the British ship *Serapis* for the United States. During the early stages of the $3\frac{1}{2}$-hour battle, the British asked him to surrender.

Find out his famous response.

September 24

Jim Henson was born on September 24, 1936. As the creator of the Muppets, Jim Henson revolutionized children's educational television.

In his honor, put on a puppet show that teaches a lesson to a young child.

September 25

Yosemite National Park was established on September 25, 1890.

Write a paragraph explaining why you do or do not think that national parks are important.

September 26

On September 26, 1820, Daniel Boone died. He helped blaze a trail through the Cumberland Gap.

Draw a map that includes the Cumberland Trail. Assess the importance of that trail.

September 27

On September 27, 1792, George Cruikshank was born. He was an artist, caricaturist, and illustrator. His most famous illustrations were for novelist Charles Dickens. He illustrated *Sketches by Boz* and *Oliver Twist*.

Define "caricature." In honor of George Cruikshank, draw a caricature of a well-known person.

September 28

The birthday of Confucius is celebrated on September 28. His teachings were the base curriculum in China for more than 2,000 years!

Put the following excerpts from his teachings into your own words and tell whether or not you agree:
"The superior man is concerned with virtue; the inferior man is concerned with land."
"The superior man understands what is right; the inferior man understands what is profitable."

10

September 29

Enrico Fermi was born on September 29, 1901. This Italian Nobel Prize winner worked on the atomic bomb project at Los Alamos, NM.

Create a poster regarding the use of nuclear weapons.

September 30

On September 30, 1927, baseball great Babe Ruth broke his own world record of 59 home runs in a season by hitting his 60th home run. This record stood until 1961.

Who beat Babe Ruth's record? Babe Ruth died in 1948. If he had been alive, how do you think he would have felt?

October 1

On this date in 1909 Henry Ford introduced the Model T to the public. He is said to have "put America on wheels." How would your life be different if starting tomorrow there were no automobiles?

October 2

Nat Turner was born on this day in 1800. Create a wanted poster for Nat Turner.

11

October 3

On this date in 1838 Sauk Chief Black Hawk died. He was 71 years of age. Summarize the causes and effects of the Black Hawk War.

October 4

Frederic Remington was born on October 4, 1861. Write a publicity article for an upcoming exhibit of his works.

October 5

Tecumseh, a Shawnee chief, died on October 5, 1913. Tecumseh was a great orator. As Tecumseh, write a speech advocating your position.

October 6

Thomas Edison showed the first full-length talking movie on this date in 1889. It was *The Jazz Singer*, starring Al Joelson. In honor of this event, write a review of a movie you have seen. Tell why you would or would not recommend it to others.

12

October 7

Marian Anderson became the first black singer hired by the Metropolitan Opera of New York City on October 7, 1954. In 1939 Ms. Anderson was to sing in Constitution Hall in Washington, D.C., but the Daughters of the American Revolution refused to allow her to appear because of her race; First Lady Eleanor Roosevelt resigned from the D.A.R. and arranged for her to give a concert on the steps of the Lincoln Memorial. Write a letter to Eleanor Roosevelt commending her for her actions.

October 8

Argentinian leader Juan Perón was born on October 8, 1895. Draw a map of Argentina. Include the capital, boundaries, and important geographical features.

October 9

Chicago was in blazes on this date in 1871. The fire started in the O'Learys' barn. Legend tells us that the cow kicked over the kerosene lantern. Think of another way the fire might have started. Write a short story.

October 10

Children's author/illustrator James Marshall was born on October 10, 1942. Obtain one of his books and read it to a younger child. Tell whether or not the child enjoyed the book.

13

October 11

Eleanor Roosevelt, wife of President Franklin Delano Roosevelt, was born on October 9, 1884. In her honor, write a job description for a first lady.

October 12

Elmer Ambrose Sperry was born October 12, 1860. He is best known for his invention of the gyrocompass. Find out what made the gyrocompass different from other compasses.

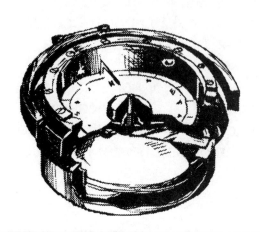

October 13

Mary McCauly was born on October 13, 1754. Draw a picture that shows how she helped during the Revolutionary War. Judge her nickname.

October 14

William Penn was born on October 14, 1644. In 1682 he was granted a charter for the territory west of the river between New York and Maryland. It was named Pennsylvania after his father, an admiral in the British navy. As someone living in Pennsylvania, write a letter to a relative in England. Tell your relative what makes the government of the territory special for its time.

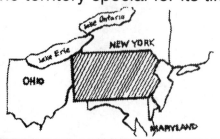

14

October 15

The television show *I Love Lucy* premiered on this date in 1951. In its honor create the premise for a new situation comedy series. Who will be its intended audience? Who will star? What day and at what time will it be broadcast?

October 16

John Brown's raid upon the Federal arsenal at Harpers Ferry, Virginia, took place on October 16, 1859. Write an editorial for a newspaper of the time.

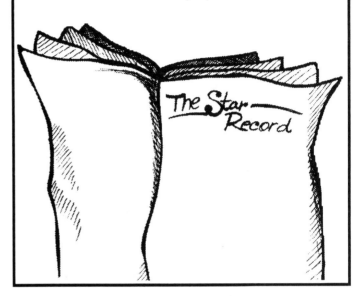

October 17

On October 17, 1777, British General Burgoyne was forced to surrender his troops at Saratoga, New York. Many historians call this the turning point in the Revolutionary War. Create a chart that explains why.

October 18

Find out what happened on October 18, 1867. Explain what is meant by Seward's Folly.

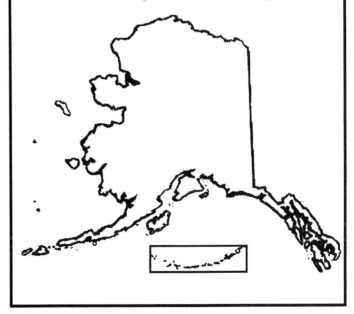

October 19

General Cornwallis surrendered to General Washington at Yorktown, Virginia, on October 19, 1781. Although fighting continued for another year, the defeat of the British at Yorktown showed that the end of the war was near. Research and find out how the Marquis de Lafayette indirectly helped the Americans win at Yorktown.

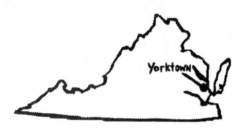

October 20

Baseball great Mickey Mantle was born on October 20, 1931. Write an acrostic poem about baseball.

October 21

Alfred Nobel was born on October 21, 1833. He made a fortune because of his patents on dynamite and other, even more powerful explosives. How did he use his wealth to benefit humankind? Surmise why he used his wealth in this manner.

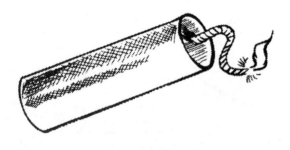

October 22

On October 22,1836, Sam Houston became the first president of Texas, which had just won its independence from Mexico. He later became one of its two U.S. senators. He was also governor of the state, but in March 1861 he was declared deposed from office. Find out why.

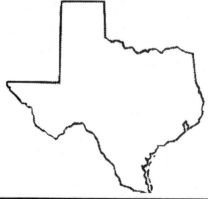

16

October 23

Pelé (Edson Arantes de Nascimiento) was born on October 23, 1940. He is probably the best known soccer player of all time. Pelé was loved so in his native Brazil that he became a national hero. Create a poster to encourage boys and girls to sign up for your local soccer league.

October 24

Anton van Leeuwenhoek was born on October 24, 1632, in Delft, Holland. He is often called the "Father of Microbiology." Draw a diagram of a compound microscope. Explain why images in a compound microscope appear upside down and backwards.

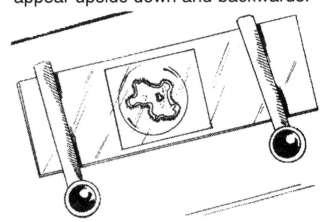

October 25

Polar explorer Richard Byrd was born October 25, 1888. Write three questions you would like to ask Richard Byrd if he were still alive. (He died in 1957.)

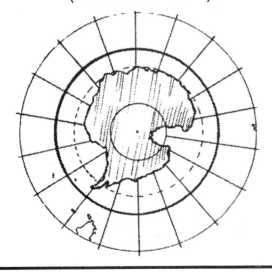

October 26

The New York Public Library was founded in 1895. Today, libraries often need the financial support of the citizens to help them meet their needs. Plan a fund raiser for your local library. Create a brochure advertising this event.

17

October 27

Theodore Roosevelt, the twenty-sixth President of the United States, was born on October 27, 1858. He was very interested in wildlife conservation. In his honor create a poster to urge the protection of endangered species of animals.

October 28

World-renowned French chef Auguste Escoffier was born on October 28, 1846. He was known as "the king of chefs and the chef of kings." In his honor plan a dinner menu fit for a king and a queen.

October 29

James Boswell was born on October 29, 1740. He is best known for his biography of Samuel Johnson. Johnson was one of the most highly regarded writers of 18th-century England. In Boswell's honor, write a brief biography of someone you know.

October 30

On October 30, 1938, Orson Welles moved thousands of listeners to near-panic with his simulated news broadcast of H.G. Wells's *War of the Worlds.* Although he prefaced his broadcast with a statement that what was about to be heard was a dramatization, many believed it to be a real report of an invasion of New Jersey by Martians. Create a conversation between a man who has just heard the report on the radio and his family who has not.

October 31

Harry Houdini died on October 31, 1926. Create a fitting epitaph for his gravestone.

November 1

November 1 is Author's Day. Many famous authors were born in November. Louisa May Alcott, Robert Louis Stevenson, Jonathan Swift, Mark Twain, C.S. Lewis, Madeleine L'Engle, and Francis Hodgson Burnett were all born in this month. Write a letter to one of them or to your favorite author telling him or her why you admire his or her work.

November 2

Find out what made November 12, 1920, different from previous presidential elections.

November 3

The Earl of Sandwich was born in London on this date in 1718. He was a gambler who sometimes found it hard to leave the gaming table. Putting meat between two slices of bread seemed the perfect solution. In honor of his birthday, create an original sandwich. Describe the bread, filling, and dressing you will use. Give your sandwich a name.

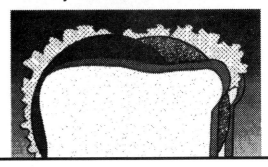

November 4

Will Rogers was born on this date in 1879. He was known both for his rope-throwing ability and his humor—especially political humor. Rogers used to say, "My folks didn't come over on the *Mayflower,* but they were there to meet the boat!" Find out what he meant by that statement.

November 5

On November 5, 1733, John Peter Zenger published the first issue of the *New York Weekly Journal.* When he published articles criticizing the policies of Governor William Cosby, he was arrested for libel. Zenger remained in prison for about 10 months. Find out why the outcome of his trial was an important step toward the establishment of freedom of the press from censorship.

November 6

John Philip Sousa was born on November 6, 1854, in Washington, D.C. Find out his nickname and tell whether or not he deserved this title.

November 7

On this date in 1805, the Lewis and Clark Expedition sighted the Pacific Ocean. Map the route taken by Lewis and Clark. Begin with their start up the Missouri River on May 14, 1804, and end with their arrival at the mouth of the Columbia River on November 15, 1805. Create a map legend to show how they travelled from place to place.

20

November 8

Swiss psychologist Hermann Rorschach was born on November 8, 1884. In 1911, he devised the inkblot test. The subject describes what he or she sees in 10 inkblots. Make your own inkblot pictures. Put some ink on a white paper. Fold the paper and rub it. Unfold it. Ask people to describe what they see.

November 9

Benjamin Banneker was born on November 9, 1731. His mother was a free woman and his father a slave; therefore, he was born free. Write a speech honoring Banneker. In your speech, list at least three of his accomplishments.

November 10

Henry Wadsworth Longfellow's poem *The Song of Hiawatha* was published in book form on November 10, 1855. It soon sold a million copies, a rare feat for a poetry book. Read *The Song of Hiawatha*. Then read about Hiawatha according to Indian tradition. Write an acrostic poem honoring the real Hiawatha.

November 11

On November 11, 1647, the first compulsory school law was passed by Massachusetts. It ordered any town of 100 or more families to set up a grammar school. Compare school education and home-schooling. List the advantages and disadvantages of each.

21

November 12

Elizabeth Cady Stanton was born on November 12, 1815. Design a plaque to honor Mrs. Stanton. Write an inscription that summarizes her major accomplishments.

November 13

Union general Joseph Hooker was born on November 13, 1814. He was in command at the Battle of Chancellorsville (May 1–4, 1863). In spite of having more than twice as many men, Hooker was outmaneuvered by General Lee, and the Union troops were defeated. The Confederates, however, suffered a great loss as a result of the battle. Find out what their loss was.

November 14

Robert Fulton was born on November 14, 1765. Design a postage stamp in his honor. The stamp should tell in words or picture something about an outstanding accomplishment.

November 15

The Second Continental Congress adopted the Articles of Confederation on November 15, 1777. From 1781 to 1789 it served as the first constitution of the new nation. Research and find out the weaknesses of the Articles of Confederation. Chart the weaknesses.

22

November 16

Maize, or corn, was found by 16 Pilgrims on November 16, 1620, in Provincetown, Massachusetts. Brainstorm all the things you can make with both the edible and inedible parts of corn. Stretch your imagination and try to think of some unusual uses.

November 17

On November 17, 1851, the first postage stamps depicting the American eagle were issued. (They were 1-cent stamps.) The bald eagle has been the U.S. national bird since 1782. Judge the choice of this bird. Would you have chosen another?

November 18

On November 18, 1894, the *New York World* published the first colored cartoon section in a Sunday newspaper. It was a 6-box cartoon, the first in a series by cartoonist Richard Felton Outcault; it was called "The Origin of a New Species." It later published his series called "Yellow Kid."
Create a 6-box cartoon.
Use well-known cartoon characters or create your own.

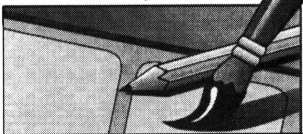

November 19

President Abraham Lincoln delivered the Gettysburg Address on November 19, 1863. The occasion was the dedication of a national cemetery on the battle-field site. The speech has been called the greatest English prose poem of modern times. As a newspaper reporter of that period of time, report on the speech. What part of the speech was most meaningful to you?

23

November 20

On November 20, 1789, New Jersey became the first state to ratify the Bill of Rights. Create a Bill of Rights for Pets.

November 21

On November 21, 1620, the *Mayflower Compact* was signed by 41 of the male passengers on the *Mayflower*. It was signed shortly before they landed at Plymouth, Massachusetts. As one of those signers, write a letter to a friend back home. Your letter should explain what the *Mayflower Compact* was and why you signed it.

November 22

On November 22, 1963, President John F. Kennedy was assassinated. One of his best known quotes comes from his inaugural address: "And so, my fellow Americans, ask not what your country can do for you—ask what you can do for your country."
In President Kennedy's memory, create a poster showing something you can do—now or in later years—for your country.

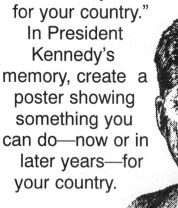

November 23

Author Roald Dahl died on this date in 1990. In his memory create an annotated bibliography of his writings for children. Read one of the books.

24

November 24

Zachary Taylor, the twelfth President of the United States, was born on November 24, 1784. Find out his nickname.

November 25

On this date in 1946 children's author/illustrator Marc Brown was born. Marc Brown is best known for his Arthur books. Read *Arthur's Thanksgiving.* Prepare a lesson for a younger class using that book.

November 26

November 26, 1789, was proclaimed a day of general thanksgiving. Can you guess what the nation had to be thankful for in 1789?

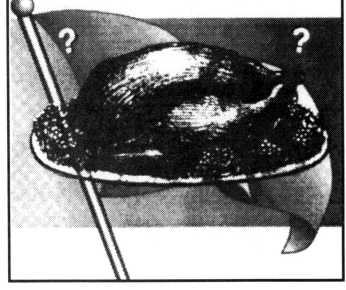

November 27

On November 27, 1960, Gordon Howe became the first hockey player to score more than 1,000 points in a regular season. Write a poem in his honor.

November 28

On November 28, 1964, *Mariner 4* was launched from Cape Kennedy, Florida. On July 14, 1965, when the satellite was 134 million miles away from Earth, it transmitted an extraordinary photograph. Draw a picture or chart that shows what *Mariner 4* photographed.

November 29

Louisa May Alcott was born on November 29, 1832. Her classic novel *Little Women* was based on the lives of Louisa and her sisters. Write a short story about an event from your childhood.

November 30

Samuel Clemens was born on November 30, 1835. It wasn't until he was in his late twenties and a writer for the *Virginia City Enterprise* that he began to use the name Mark Twain. Find out what the name means. What name would you choose if you wanted a pen name? Why?

December 1

Madame Tussaud was born on December 1, 1761. She founded Madame Tussaud's exhibition of life-like figures in London. The exhibition includes all types of characters, both famous and infamous. For example, notorious criminals are "housed" together in the Chamber of Horrors. You are in charge of planning a new room, the Chambers of Heroes and Heroines. What 10 people, past or present, will you include?

26

December 2

On this date in 1823 President James Monroe made a proclamation that later became known as the Monroe Doctrine. Although it had little immediate effect, by World War I it had become an important tenet of U.S. foreign policy. List the three basic principles of the Monroe Doctrine.

December 3

On December 3, 1967, Dr. Christian Barnard performed breakthrough surgery. Find out the nature of the surgery.

December 4

MOULTRIE FORT

William Moultrie was born on this date in 1730. Fort Moultrie in South Carolina is named for him. Find out why.

December 5

The 21st amendment was ratified on December 5, 1933. Draw a poster that shows the effect of that amendment.

21 ST AMENDMENT

27

December 6

Joyce Kilmer was born in New Brunswick, New Jersey, on December 6, 1886. He is best known for his poem "Trees." Kilmer was killed in action during World War I. In his honor compose a cinquain about a tree or other form of nature that you admire.

December 7

President Franklin Delano Roosevelt called this day in 1941 "a date which will live in infamy." What happened on this date to cause him to say this?

December 8

Eli Whitney was born on December 8, 1765. He is famous for his invention of the cotton gin; however, he made an even more important contribution to the manufacture of firearms. Design a plaque honoring him for this contribution.

December 9

Circus clown Emmett Kelly is remembered for his role as Weary Willie, a mournful tramp. He had created Willie as a cartoon character before bringing him to life in the circus. In honor of Kelly's birthday create your own clown cartoon character. Draw a picture and write a paragraph about him or her.

28

December 10

Alfred Nobel died on December 10, 1896. He was a chemist, engineer, and industrialist. He invented dynamite and other, more powerful explosives. Nobel is better known, however, for his philanthropic contributions. Create a newspaper headline for December 10th that tells something about Nobel's interest in bettering society.

December 11

Prince Edward, duke of Windsor, was king of Great Britain and Ireland as King Edward VIII from January 20 to December 10, 1936, when he abdicated, or gave up, the throne. Find out why he abdicated. Then create three questions you might have asked him if you had had the chance to interview him.

December 12

John Jay, the first Chief Justice of the United States Supreme Court, was born on December 12, 1745. In 1787 Jay, using the pseudonym "Publius," wrote five essays for *The Federalist*. Explain the purpose of *The Federalist*.

December 13

Yehudi Menuhin debuted at Carnegie Hall on December 13, 1926. Research his life and decide whether or not the term *child prodigy* aptly describes him.

December 14

On this date in 1911, Norwegian explorer Roald Amundsen became the first human to reach the South Pole. If you could be the first at something, what would it be?

December 15

French bridge engineer Alexandre-Gustave Eiffel was born on this date in 1832. He is best known for the tower in Paris that is named for him. It was the tallest building in the world, took only a few months to raise, and was relatively inexpensive. The Eiffel Tower remained the tallest building in the world until 1939 when the Chrysler Building in New York City was completed. Create a travel brochure for a world monument you would like to visit.

December 16

The first children's museum, the Brooklyn Children's Museum, opened on December 16, 1899. Describe an exhibit you would like to see in a museum.

December 17

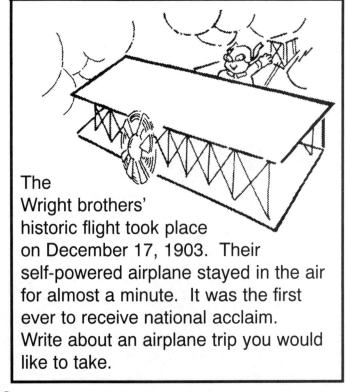

The Wright brothers' historic flight took place on December 17, 1903. Their self-powered airplane stayed in the air for almost a minute. It was the first ever to receive national acclaim. Write about an airplane trip you would like to take.

30

December 18

Renowned Italian violin maker Antonio Stradivari died on this date in 1737. Many consider his violins to be perfect instruments. In his memory, create a musical-instrument word search.

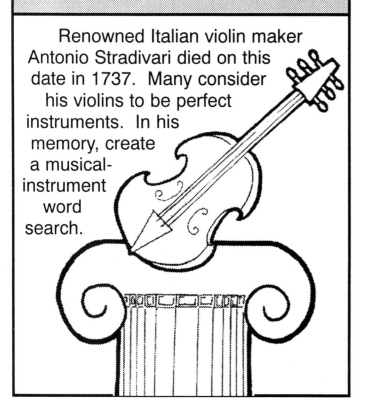

December 19

The first radio broadcast from outer space was made on December 19, 1958. A tape recording of President Eisenhower's Christmas message was broadcast from a rocket revolving around the earth. If you could have a message broadcast from outer space, what would you say to the people of Earth? Make your message 50 words or less.

December 20

Shortly after Abraham Lincoln was elected President of the United States, South Carolina called a convention. The results of that convention were announced on December 20, 1860. That announcement shook the nation! Explain why.

December 21

On this date in 1913 the first crossword puzzle was published. It was prepared by Arthur Wynne and was published in the supplement of the Sunday edition of the New York *World*. In honor of this occasion and of the first day of winter, create a crossword puzzle with a winter theme.

31

December 22

(Helen) Beatrix Potter was born in England on July 28, 1866, and died on December 22, 1943. This beloved children's author and illustrator is best known for her animal stories. List at least three of those stories.

December 23

Jean-François Champollion, French historian and linguist, was born on December 23, 1790. He is best known for his work with the Rosetta Stone. Research the Rosetta Stone and find out why it was important.

December 24

On January 8, 1815, American troops led by Andrew Jackson defeated British forces at the Battle of New Orleans. The battle made Jackson a hero, but it was an unnecessary battle. Find out why it was unnecessary.

December 25

Clara Barton was born on this date in 1821. Find out how this former school teacher earned the nickname "Angel of the Battlefield."

32

December 26

December 26 is Boxing Day in Great Britain, Canada, and some other Commonwealth nations. It is a day to show appreciation to those who have performed personal public services during the year. Design a card to include in a gift to a mail carrier or another public servant. Find out how the name Boxing Day originated.

December 27

German astronomer Johannes Kepler was born on December 27, 1751. Draw a chart that shows Kepler's major discovery.

December 28

William Simple of Mount Vernon, Ohio, was granted a patent for chewing gum in 1869. An acrostic poem is one in which the first letter of each line spells a name or other word. Create an acrostic about chewing gum.

December 29

President Andrew Johnson was born on December 29, 1808. Congress wanted him out of office and, therefore, voted to impeach him. He was the first President ever to be impeached; however, he was not convicted and, therefore, remained in office. Define impeachment. Do you think Congress should have the ability to impeach a President?

33

December 30

Rudyard Kipling was born on December 30, 1865. He received the Nobel Prize for Literature in 1907. Create a poster advertising a book or poem by Rudyard Kipling.

December 31

Baseball great Roberto Clemente died on December 31, 1972, at the age of forty-two. In 1973 he was elected to the Baseball Hall of Fame. Roberto Clemente was more than just a great baseball player, however. Use the circumstances of his death to explain his greatness. Design a plaque in his memory.

January 1

On January 1, 1863, President Lincoln issued the Emancipation Proclamation. Compare and contrast the Emancipation Proclamation and the Thirteenth Amendment to the Constitution.

January 2

Nathaniel Bacon was born in Suffolk, England, on January 2, 1647. Find out what is meant by Bacon's Rebellion.

34

January 3

The first free kindergarten opened on January 3, 1876. Classes were held in the home of its founder, Samuel Lapham Hill. In its honor plan a lesson to teach kindergarten children about sequencing events.

January 4

French educator Louis Braille was born on January 4, 1809, and died on January 6, 1852. Find out what is meant by the Braille system. As someone who uses his system, write a letter thanking him and explaining how it has benefitted you.

January 5

Stephen Decatur, naval hero of the War of 1812, was born on January 5, 1779. Complete this famous quotation made by Decatur: "Our country!... may she always be in the right; _____."
To solve, take the correct path on the puzzle grid.

start ↓	O	U	I	G	H
B	C	N	R	O	T
U	R	T	,	R	W
T	U	R	Y	N	R
O	THE END	.	G	O

January 6

Carl Sandburg was born in Illinois on January 6, 1878. He was a poet, historian, novelist, and folklorist. His most famous poem was "Chicago." Sandburg was known as a "poet of the common people." In honor of his birth date write a poem with an ordinary person or ordinary people as its theme.

January 7

On January 7, 1955, Marian Anderson sang at the Metropolitan Opera House in New York City. Find out why this was a special event.

January 8

Solve this riddle to find out who was born on this date in 1935.
1. I was a rock-and-roll singer.
2. I was born in Tupelo, Mississippi.
3. My nickname is "The King of Rock and Roll."
4. My home was called Graceland.

January 9

The Seeing Eye was incorporated on January 9, 1929. Design an award that honors the Seeing Eye and describes the service the organization performs.

SEEING EYE, INC.

January 10

On January 10, 1977, President Ford presented the Medal of Freedom to Will and Ariel Durant. It was the first time a married couple was awarded this medal. They received it for their Pulitzer Prize-winning *The Story of Civilization.* Find out what the Medal of Freedom is. Write a letter to the President nominating someone for this honor.

36

January 11

Alexander Hamilton was born on January 11, 1757, in Jamaica, West Indies. He was one of the three signers of the Declaration of Independence from the state of New York. He also is known for his contribution to the *Federalist Papers.* Write a paragraph explaining what is meant by the *Federalist Papers.*

January 12

Jack London was born on January 12, 1876. This classic novelist and short-story writer is best known for his stories of survival. His most famous work, *The Call of the Wild,* tells of the adaptability of Buck, a dog forced to live in the wild. In honor of London's birthday, create a plot for a story of survival.

January 13

Horatio Alger was born on January 13, 1832. He was one of the most popular American authors during the last thirty years of the nineteenth century. Find out what was characteristic of his plots. Create a plot in his style.

STREET LIFE IN NEW YORK BY HORATIO ALGER

January 14

Benedict Arnold was born on January 14, 1741. Although he was a fine officer and a loyal Patriot until 1789, his name then became synonymous with "traitor." As Benedict Arnold, write a letter to an acquaintance back in America. In it explain what you did and why.

37

January 15

Matthew Brady died on this date in 1896. Ironically, the project which brought him the greatest fame also caused him financial ruin. Create a poster announcing an exhibit of his works. Give a title to the exhibit.

January 16

Dian Fossey was born on January 16, 1932. She devoted many years of her life to the study of gorillas in the wild. If you could study any animal in the world, which would you choose? Why?

January 17

Muhammad Ali was born on January 17, 1942. He made "I am the greatest!" his personal slogan. Another of his famous sayings is "float like a butterfly, sting like a bee."
Create a simile that describes you.

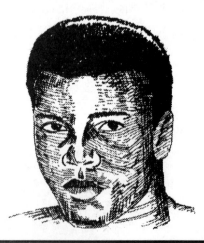

January 18

Daniel Webster, one of the most eloquent orators of all time, was born on January 18, 1782. He was a staunch defender of the powers of the federal government as opposed to states' rights. One of his best known speeches ended with "Liberty and Union, now and forever, one and inseparable!" Think about something you care deeply about. Write a speech setting forth your point of view.

38

January 19

Edgar Allan Poe was born on January 19, 1809. He is credited with being the creator of detective fiction. Read a detective story or other mystery. Tell why you would or would not recommend it to a friend.

January 20

Beloved entertainer George Burns was born on January 20, 1896, and died on March 9, 1996! His career included vaudeville, radio, television, and film. He was about 80 years of age when he won an Academy Award for his supporting role in *The Sunshine Boys!* Write a poem in honor of George Burns.

January 21

John C. Frémont was born on January 21, 1813. He has been nick-named the "Pathfinder." Research his life. Write at least three facts that could be used to support the appropriateness of that nickname.

January 22

The first postal route was between New York City and Boston, Massachusetts. The first trip was made on January 22, 1673. As a 1673 resident of New York City, write a letter to someone living in Boston. Write about your daily life.

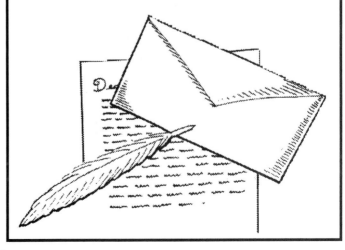

39

January 23

On this date in 1849 Elizabeth Blackwell accomplished a special achievement. Design a plaque that honors this special feat.

January 24

Of Osage descent, Maria Tallchief was born on January 24, 1925, in Fairfax, Oklahoma. Unscramble these words to find out the reason for her fame.

AIRPM IELABLRNA

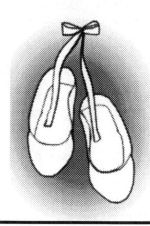

January 25

Robert Burns, Scotland's national poet, was born on January 25, 1759. He died on July 21, 1796. One of the most beloved poets of all time, his birthday is still celebrated heartily by his fellow countrymen. Burns is best known for his songs, which he wrote to known tunes. In honor of "Bobby" Burns, write a song. Set it to a known tune.

January 26

The man who is credited with the following quotations was born on January 26, 1880: "I shall return." "In war there is no substitute for victory." "Old soldiers never die; they just fade away." Find out who said these things and under what circumstances.

40

January 27

Charles Dodgson, better known as Lewis Carroll, was born on February 27, 1832. He was the author of *Alice's Adventures in Wonderland* and *Through the Looking-Glass and What Alice Found There.* He was also the author of humorous poems, such as "Jabberwocky." The term "jabberwocky" is now used to describe nonsense speech or writing meant to appear to make sense. Carroll's poem was made up of portmanteau words. Find out what that means and create two new ones.

January 28

Sir Francis Drake, considered by many to be the greatest English seaman of the Elizabethan Age, died on January 28, 1596. He was about 56–59 years of age. Research his life and create an acrostic poem about him.

January 29

Thomas Paine, one of the greatest political pamphleteers in history, was born on this date in 1737. Judge his importance to the Patriot cause.

January 30

Franklin Delano Roosevelt was born on January 30, 1882. He was the only person to hold the office of President of the United States more than twice. The 22nd Amendment made it unconstitutional. FDR died during his fourth term. Use your imagination and think of other possible things "FDR" could stand for. Draw or act out your ideas. Have your classmates guess the meanings.

EXAMPLE:
FIVE DANCING RABBITS

41

January 31

Robert Morris was born on this date in 1734. Gouverneur Morris was born on this date in 1752. They were not related; however, they shared something very important (in addition to their birthday)! Find out what else they shared!

February 1

On this date in 1978 a U.S. postage stamp honoring Harriet Tubman was issued. It was the first time a black woman was so honored. Write a sentence explaining what she did to earn this honor.

February 2

Musical prodigy Jascha Heifitz was born on February 2, 1901, in Lithuania. He toured Europe from the age of 12! Draw a picture of the instrument for which he is known.

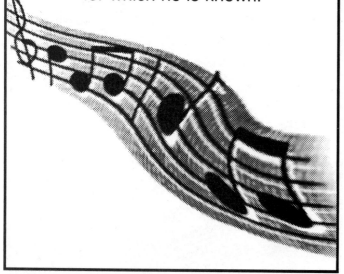

February 3

Horace Greeley, founder of the *New York Tribune,* was born on February 3, 1811. He gained a reputation as the most outstanding editor of his time. Greeley is best known for his uncompromising antislavery editorials. Read an editorial in a recent edition of a newspaper. Tell why you agree or disagree with the editor.

February 4

Rosa Parks was born on February 4, 1913. This black seamstress changed the course of history on December 1, 1955, when she was arrested for taking a seat in the white section of the bus. Create a newspaper headline that tells what event resulted from her arrest.

February 5

Baseball Hall-of-Famer Hank Aaron was born on February 5, 1934. He began his professional career in the Negro American League. After only a few months, however, he entered the major leagues, where he remained for 23 seasons! He broke many records! Design a T-shirt honoring the record for which he is best known.

February 6

George Herman Ruth was born on this date in 1895. He's better known as Babe Ruth. He was one of the first five players elected into the Hall of Fame in 1936. Unscramble these words to find out his nickname.

USLATN
FO TWSA

February 7

Laura Ingalls Wilder was born on this date in 1867. The books she wrote were based on her youth in the Midwest and in the Dakotas. List at least 3 of her books. Read one of them and tell why you would or would not like to have grown up during that period of time.

43

February 8

Boy Scouts of America, an organization for boys nine and over, was incorporated on this date in 1910. Its motto is Be Prepared. Create a poster that illustrates an important way in which a person (male or female) can be prepared at home, at school, at work, or at play.

February 9

On February 9, 1861, Jefferson Davis was elected President of the Confederacy. He tried to keep the war going even after General Lee's surrender; however, he was captured on May 10, 1865, and imprisoned for two years. He was indicted for treason, but the case was dropped on December 25,1868. Do you think Davis would have been convicted? Explain.

February 10

The Treaty of Paris was signed on this date in 1763. Name the conflict ended by this treaty and the parties involved. Summarize the reason for the conflict. Which party was victorious?

February 11

On this date in 1990, Nelson Mandela was released from the South African prison where he had been held for 27 years. As Mandela, write an entry in your diary telling how you felt upon being freed.

44

February 12

John L. Lewis was born on February 12, 1880. He was president of the UMWA from 1920 to 1960. As a committee leader in the AFL, he organized mass-production workers into industrial unions. When these unions were expelled from the AFL, they were re-established as the CIO. Lewis, the chief founder of the CIO, became its president. In 1940 he resigned from the CIO and in 1942 he pulled the UMWA out of that organization. What do these acronyms stand for:

UMWA, AFL, and CIO?

February 13

Although they all died within 2 weeks, the first quintuplets known to have been born in America were born in Wisconsin on February 13, 1875. Write how your life would be different if you were a quintuplet. Would you like it?

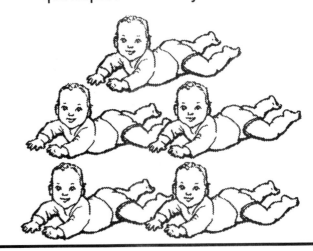

February 14

A patent was given for an apple parer on this date in 1803. Can you think of something you would like to invent? How would it make your or someone else's life easier?

February 15

Susan B. Anthony was born on February 15, 1820. Her work helped pave the way for passage of the Nineteenth Amendment to the United States Constitution. Explain.

45

February 16

The first Esperanto Club was organized on this date in 1905. Explain what is meant by Esperanto.

February 17

The National Congress of Mothers, the first national parent-teacher association, was organized on February 17, 1897. Today that organization is known as the National Congress of Parents and Teachers or PTA for short. Is your local parent-teacher association affiliated with this organization? Write a letter to your local parent-teacher organization thanking them for something they have done to help your school.

February 18

An important astronomical discovery was made on this date in 1930. What was it?

February 19

The *Monitor* was completed on February 19, 1862. Explain the significance of the naval battle that took place between the Union *Monitor* and the Confederate *Merrimack* on March 9, 1862.

46

February 20

On February 20, 1962, John H. Glenn, Jr., made history. Write a headline for a newspaper that announces his accomplishment.

February 21

Spanish guitarist Andrés Segovia was born on this date in 1893. In his honor, create a Musical Instrument Word Search.

February 22

American poet Edna St. Vincent Millay was born on this date in 1950. Much of her work was done in sonnet form. Write rules to follow in creating the English form of the sonnet.

February 23

Famous English diarist Samuel Pepys (pēps) was born on February 23, 1633. He began his diary in January 1660 and ended it on May 31, 1669. Many important events in English history were recorded in it. Create an entry in your diary in which you record one or more political and social events and customs of your time.

47

February 24

Wilhelm Grimm was born in Germany on February 24, 1786. He and his brother Jacob are known for their collection of folk tales, which they had transcribed from oral sources. Read *Hansel and Gretel, Rapunzel, Rumpelstiltskin,* or another story retold by the Grimm brothers. Then read a different version of the same tale. Compare the two.

February 25

On this date in 1913, the 16th Amendment was ratified. What power did this amendment give to Congress?

February 26

"Buffalo Bill" Cody was born on February 26, 1846. He was a buffalo hunter, U.S. army scout, and Indian fighter. His Wild West Show became known worldwide. Research his life and write a clerihew in his honor.

February 27

On this date in 1795 Francis Marion died. Find out his nickname and how he got it.

48

February 28

British illustrator Sir John Tenniel was born on February 28, 1820. He is best known for his political cartoons drawn for the periodical *Punch* and for his illustrations for *Alice in Wonderland* * and *Through the Looking Glass.* Create a political cartoon.

*Artist's rendering of Tenniel's "The Mad Hatter" from *Alice in Wonderland*.

February 29

Today is Leap Year Day. How would you feel if your birthday came only every four years? If your birthday really is February 29, tell how it feels.

Happy Birthday! FEB. 29th

March 1

Come to See!

Yellowstone National Park, the first national park, was authorized on March 1, 1872. Create an advertisement for the travel section of the newspaper. Your ad should encourage tourists to visit the park. Include in word or picture a description of its most famous attraction.

March 2

Sam Houston led the U.S. settlers in Texas in their rebellion against Mexico. With a force of less than 800 men, he defeated about 1,600 Mexicans under General Antonio López de Santa Anna at San Jacinto. This victory led to Texan independence. Houston was also instrumental in gaining the annexation of Texas by the United States in 1845. He served as U.S. senator from 1846 to 1859 and in 1859 was elected governor. Find out why he was deposed from office in March 1861.

March 3

Alexander Graham Bell was born in Edinburgh, Scotland, on March 3, 1847.
On March 7, 1876, the U.S. Patent Office granted him a patent for his invention of the telephone.
Write a story in which you describe how your life would be different if the tele- phone had not been invented.

March 4

Knute Rockne was born on March 4, 1888. This world-famous football coach served as head coach from 1918–1930.

Unscramble the letters to determine the nickname of Rockne's team.

HTE FGIHTNIG RIIHS

March 5

Crispus Attucks and four others were killed on March 5, 1770, when British soldiers fired at a taunting crowd. What is this incident now called?

March 6

The Alamo was an 18th-century Franciscan mission in San Antonio, Texas. During the fight for Texan independence from Mexico, the Alamo became a symbol of the spirit of resistance. Explain what is meant by the battle cry "Remember the Alamo!"

50

March 7

Luther Burbank was born on March 7, 1849, in Lancaster, Massachusetts. In his lifetime, this remarkably successful plant breeder developed more than 800 new strains and varieties of plants!
In his honor create a fruit-and-vegetable word search!

March 8

Oliver Wendell Holmes, Jr., was born in Boston on March 8, 1841. In 1902 he was appointed by President Theodore Roosevelt to the United States Supreme Court. He remained on the court for 30 years, retiring just before his 91st birthday! Explain his concept of "clear and present danger" regarding free speech.

March 9

Chess master Bobby Fischer was born on March 9, 1943, in Chicago. In 1958 he became the youngest player ever to attain the rank of grand master. Find out what achievement he attained in 1972.
Design an award honoring his achievement.

March 10

Wilt Chamberlain was the first professional basketball player to score over 32,000 points in one season. On March 10, 1961, he scored 32 points, bringing his total to 3,033 for 79 games.

The next year he became the first player to score more than 4,000 points in a season? Create a clerihew about Wilt Chamberlain.

51

March 11

British bacteriologist Sir Alexander Fleming was born on March 11, 1955. In 1945 he shared the Nobel Prize for Physiology or Medicine. Find out what he discovered and with whom he shared the honor.

March 12

British army captain Charles Boycott was born on March 12, 1832. His name became the noun and verb "boycott." See if you can find out why it was named for him.

March 13

Today is my (Rebecca Stark's) birthday. Although I do not believe in astrology, I do occasionally check my horoscope just for fun. I'm a Pisces.

Under which sign were you born? Check your horoscope in the newspaper.

March 14

Albert Einstein was born in Germany on March 14, 1879. He is regarded as one of the most creative geniuses of all time. He is best known for his theory of relativity. Solve the puzzle and find out what "relativity" is.

START HERE	A	N	A	P	P
D	Y	O	F	T	R
U	P	A	C	I	O
T	S	END HERE	E	M	A
S	D	N	A	E	C
E	H	T	O	T	H

52

March 15

In the ancient Roman calendar, the 15th day of March, May, July, or October and the 13th of the other months were called the ides. Find out what happened on the ides of March in 44 B.C. in Rome.

March 16

Neil Armstrong orbited Earth in *Gemini VIII,* which was launched on March 16, 1966. The satellite achieved the world's first docking in space when it was hoisted aboard the U.S.S. *Leonard F. Mason* the next day. Draw a picture that depicts Neil Armstrong's most famous accomplishment.

March 17

Rudolf Nureyev was born on March 17, 1938, in Russia. He died on January 6, 1993. Create a poem honoring him.

March 18

Grover Cleveland was born on March 18, 1837. His reputation for honesty even earned him the respect of his political opponents. Find out the years he served. What is unique about his terms of office?

53

March 19

Scholar and explorer Sir Richard Burton was born in England on March 19, 1821. He was the first European to discover Lake Tanganyika.

Lake Tanganyika

Locate Lake Tanganyika on a world map. Explain what makes Lake Tanganyika special.

March 20

On this date in 1954, the first vending machines to deliver a single copy of a newspaper were leased to several major newspapers. This type of machine is still available on the streets of many cities and towns. What types of vending machines not now available would you like to have available to you?

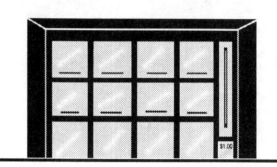

March 21

German musician Johann Sebastian Bach, generally regarded as one of the greatest musicians the world has ever known, was born on March 21, 1685. He composed an enormous number of masterpieces of church and instrumental music. Unscramble the following words and find out the instruments for which many of his works were written.

AHRSPIHCDRO

LOIVNI

LFTUE

ROAGN

March 22

On this date in 1960 the first patent on lasers was granted. The patent on "masers and maser communication system" was assigned to the Bell Telephone Laboratories in New York City. *Maser* and *laser* are both acronyms. Find out what each stands for.

March 23

On this date in 1775 a famous Patriot made a speech in which he said, "I know not what course others may take, but as for me, give me liberty or give me death." Find out who said it and where.

March 24

Create a newspaper headline for an article about the incident of March 24, 1989, involving the *Exxon Valdez*.

March 25

Gutzon Borglum was born in Idaho on March 25, 1867. This sculptor revived the ancient Egyptian and Mesopotamian practice of carving huge statues of political figures into rock. Draw a picture that illustrates his most famous work.

March 26

Sandra Day O'Connor was born on March 26, 1930, in El Paso, Texas. Pretend that it is September 26, 1981, and that you are a friend of hers. Write her a brief note congratulating her on yesterday's momentous occasion.

55

March 27

William Conrad Röntgen (Roentgen) was born in what was then Prussia on March 27, 1845. He was the first to receive the Nobel Prize for Physics (1901). Design a plaque that tells why he won this prestigious award.

March 28

On March 28, 1848, Pennsylvania approved a law prohibiting children under twelve from engaging in commercial labor. It was the first law restricting the age of a worker. As a citizen of the time, write a letter to the editor encouraging approval of that law.

March 29

John Tyler was born on March 29, 1790. Explain the circumstances under which he became the tenth President of the United States.

March 30

Vincent van Gogh was born in the Netherlands on March 30, 1853. Many consider him the greatest Dutch painter after Rembrandt. Many of his best known works were self-portraits. Paint or draw a self-portrait.

56

March 31

U.S. migrant farm worker Cesar Chavez was born in Yuma, Arizona, on March 31, 1927. He died on April 23, 1993. Research his life. Create a suitable epitaph for his tombstone.

April 1

April 1 is April Fools' Day. The custom of playing practical jokes on this date has been observed in many countries for several centuries. In France the fooled person is called a *poisson d'avril,* or April fish. In Scotland the victim is called a cuckoo. Think of an elaborate, but harmless practical joke you could play on someone. Write a paragraph describing the details of your scheme.

April 2

Danish fairy-tale writer Hans Christian Andersen, was born on April 2, 1805. Alone or with your cooperative group, create a stick-puppet skit based on one of his tales. Perform your skit for a younger audience.

April 3

Washington Irving was born on April 3, 1783, in New York City. He is known as the "inventor of the short story." One of his best known characters was Rip Van Winkle, a man who took a 20-year-long nap. Suppose someone in your town fell asleep twenty years ago and just woke up! Research and find out what would have changed. Write a story.

57

April 4

Dorothea Dix was born in Maine on April 4, 1802. Create a plaque that honors her effort to help those less fortunate than she.

April 5

Colin Powell, Chairman of the Joint Chiefs of Staff under President Bush, was born on April 5, 1937. He was the first African-American to hold this very important position. Explain what is meant by "Joint Chiefs of Staff."

April 6

The North Pole was discovered on April 6, 1909. Although Robert Peary, the leader of the expedition, is most often credited with the discovery, some believe he was not really the first to arrive at the pole. Research and find out who may have reached it first.

April 7

WHO was organized on this date in 1948. What is meant by WHO? What kind of word is *WHO?*

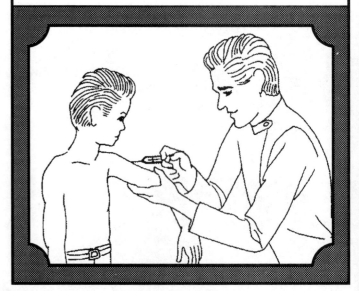

58

April 8

On April 8, 1974, the crowd stood and cheered as baseball great Hank Aaron rounded the bases. Why?

April 9

On April 9, 1963, Sir Winston Churchill, former prime minister of England, was made an honorary citizen of the United States. Use these clues to learn the identity of the man made an honorary citizen by many states in 1784.

CLUES

1. He was born in France on September 6, 1757.

2. He fought for the Americans and was made a major general during the American War for Independence.

3. He persuaded King Louis XVI to send an expeditionary army to assist the Americans.

April 10

Joseph Pulitzer was born on April 10, 1847, in Hungary. Explain what is meant by the Pulitzer Prizes.

April 11

On April 11, 1898, President McKinley made the following statement: "In the name of humanity, in the name of civilization, in behalf of endangered American interests which give us the right and duty to speak and act, the war in Cuba must stop." Under what circumstances did he make it?

59

April 12

Children's author Beverly Cleary was born on April 12, 1916. Among her best known works are those about Ramona Quimby and those about Henry Huggins. Read a book from either series. Create a plot for a new book in that series.

April 13

On April 13, 1945, Harry S. Truman made this statement to reporters: "When they told me yesterday what had happened, I felt like the moon, the stars, and all the planets had fallen on me." Explain what had happened to cause him to make that statement.

April 14

President Abraham Lincoln and his wife were enjoying a play at Ford's Theater in Washington, D.C., on April 14, 1865, when the President was fatally shot by John Wilkes Booth. Bitter about the outcome of the war, Booth shouted, *"Sic semper tyrannis!"* (This always to tyrants.) Unscramble the letters to find out what else Booth supposedly said after he shot Lincoln.

HTE TOSUH SI

VANEGED.

April 15

On April 15, 1947, Jackie Robinson made history by becoming the first black baseball player to play in the major leagues. Do you think this took courage? Explain your point of view.

60

April 16

Silent-film star Charlie Chaplin was born on April 16, 1889, in London, England. His best known character was the little tramp. Pantomime, or acting that consists mostly of gesture, is important in silent films. Alone or with your cooperative group, choose a selection from a book you have read. Pantomime an episode in that book.

April 17

Archaeologist Sir Leonard Woolley was born in London on April 7, 1880. His excavation of the ancient Sumerian city of Ur, now part of Iraq, did a lot to further our knowledge of ancient Mesopotamia. Archaeology is the systematic recovery and study of the material evidence of past human life and culture. See how many words of 3 or more letters you can form by using the letters in the word *archaeology*.

A-R-C-H-A-E-O-L-O-G-Y

April 18

On April 18, 1906, at 5:13 A.M. a severe earthquake hit San Francisco, California. Over 500 city blocks, including 28,000 buildings, were destroyed. Some estimates put the property damage as high as $500 million. About 700 people died, and about 250,000 were left homeless. Much of the damage was caused by the fire that followed the quake. San Francisco lies on the San Andreas Fault. Identify the San Andreas Fault and explain its significance.

April 19

On April 19, 1775, Captain John Parker made the following statement: "Stand your ground! Don't fire unless fired upon. But if they mean to have a war, let it begin here!" Answer these questions:

1. To whom did he say it?
2. During what battle did he say it?
3. What war was about to begin?
4. To whom did "they" refer?

61

April 20

Most consider Yellowstone National Park in Wyoming to be the first U.S. national park; however, forty years earlier, on April 20, 1832, Congress established Hot Springs, consisting of 911 acres, as a reservation. It wasn't until 1921 that it was designated Hot Springs National Park. Find out where Hot Springs is located. Explain why it is so named.

April 21

German educator Friedrich Froebel was born on April 21, 1782. He is best known as the originator and developer of kindergarten education. In his honor, prepare a lesson to teach kindergarten children about baby animals.

April 22

American humorist Erma Bombeck died on this date in 1996. She used the experiences of her life in the suburbs as the basis for her humorous columns and books. Create a plot in which you turn an everyday experience into a humorous story.

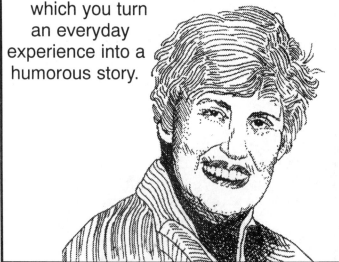

April 23

William Shakespeare was born in Stratford-on-Avon, England, on April 23, 1564. Read the following quotes. Which one is *not* attributed to William Shakespeare?

1. All the world's a stage.
2. Parting is such sweet sorrow.
3. What's in a name?
   That which we call a rose
   By any other name
   would smell as sweet.
4. In this world nothing is certain but death and taxes.

62

April 24

The Library of Congress was authorized on this date in 1800. At first housed in the Capitol, it was destroyed in 1814. In 1897 the Library of Congress moved to its permanent headquarters. Find out how the Library of Congress was destroyed.

April 25

Broadcast journalist and producer Edward R. Murrow was born on April 25, 1908, in Greensboro, North Carolina. He anchored the television series *See It Now,* which was an innovative hour-long weekly news digest. He also served as host on *Person to Person,* for which he interviewed celebrities in their homes. Choose a famous person you would like to interview. Create five questions you would ask that person.

April 26

John Jay Audubon was born in Haiti on April 26, 1785. Find out what Audubon is known for. Create a quatrain in his honor.

April 27

Animator Walter Lantz was born in New Rochelle, New York, on April 27, 1900. His most famous cartoon character was Woody Woodpecker. Woody made his debut in a bit part in the 1940 cartoon short "Knock, Knock." Lantz said that the inspiration for the character was a pesky woodpecker that disturbed his honeymoon. Create a fact file about woodpeckers; include at least five facts.

63

April 28

James Monroe, the fifth President of the United States, was born in Virginia on April 28, 1758. In 1823 he proclaimed in his presidential message what has come to be known as the Monroe Doctrine. Its principles had been prepared in part by Monroe's secretary of state, John Quincy Adams. Write a sentence that summarizes the Monroe Doctrine.

April 29

On April 29, 1913, Gideon Sundback of New Jersey obtained a patent for "separable fasteners." Today we call his invention the "zipper." The word was at first a B.F. Goodrich trademark for boots with slide fasteners; it was named for the sound it made. In time the words "zipper" and "zip" became part of the general vocabulary. "Zipper" is an example of onomatopoeia. Explain the term and give two other examples.

April 30

Railroad engineer John Luther Jones, better known as Casey Jones, died on April 30, 1900. The ballad by T. Lawrence Siebert and Eddie Newton, published in 1909, made him a national folk hero. Find out what it was about his death that led to this myth.

May 1

On this date in 1704 the first advertisements were published in a newspaper. One was a real-estate ad; one offered a reward for the capture of a thief; and one announced the loss of 2 anvils. Write an ad for the classified section of your local paper.

64

May 2

The United States signed a treaty with Napoleon of France on May 2, 1803. Draw a map that shows what the U.S. gained as a result of that treaty.

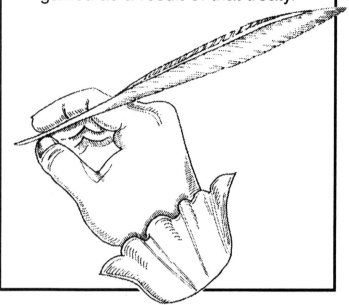

May 3

On this date in 1943 poet Robert Frost received his fourth Pulitzer Prize. Most of his verse reflected his experiences in rural New England. Create a poem that reflects life in your hometown.

May 4

On May 4, 1776, invisible ink was used for the first time in diplomatic correspondence. It was used by Silas Deane. Unscramble the message to find out the name of the organization of which he was a member.

MEEOCMITT FO CESRET
ROCRSEOPNEDNEC

May 5

Alan Shepard, Jr., made American history on this date in 1961. Design a plaque honoring his accomplishment.

65

May 6

On May 6, 1929, the first Academy Awards were presented. *Wings*, a silent film, was the first recipient. What is your favorite movie? Write an ad that a video store might use to promote the sale or rental of that film.

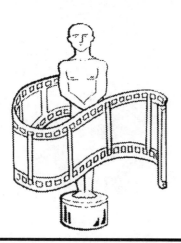

May 7

Johannes Brahms was born in Hamburg, Germany, on this date in 1833. In his honor create a Musical Instrument Word Search.

May 8

The first important dog show was held in New York City on May 8, 1877. It was sponsored by the Westminster Kennel Bench Show of Dogs. Think of as many different breeds of dogs as you can. Compare your list with those of your classmates.

May 9

John Brown was born on May 9, 1800, in Torrington, Connecticut. Define the word "martyr." Then explain why John Brown does or does not fit your definition. Name someone else you believe to have been a martyr. Explain.

66

May 10

On May 10, 1775, Ethan Allen and 83 men crossed Lake Champlain from Vermont. They entered Fort Ticonderoga while the British soldiers were asleep and succeeded in capturing the fort. What was the nickname of Allen's group of men?

May 11

Minnesota was admitted to the Union on this date in 1858, becoming the 32nd state. See how many little words (3 or more letters) you can form by using the letters in Minnesota. (Don't use the "s" to form plurals!)

May 12

Edward Lear was born on this date in 1812. Although he was an artist, he is best known for his nonsense verse— especially his limericks. Find out the rules regarding limericks.
Create an original limerick.

May 13

On May 13, 1607, 105 colonists arrived from England. They founded Jamestown, Virginia, the first permanent English settlement in America. Captain John Smith helped the settlement survive by insisting that all settlers do their share of the work. Find out how John Rolfe helped after Smith left.

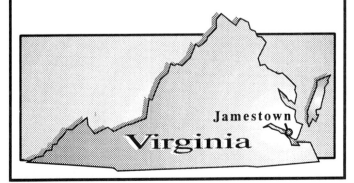

67

May 14

On May 14, 1878, the word "Vaseline" was registered as a trademark to identify a brand of petroleum jelly. It is often used to refer to the product in general. Try to think of other brand names that have come to be used to identify a product in general.

May 15

This is National Police Officers' Memorial Day. Write a poem honoring police officers in general or one in particular.

May 16

On this date in 1959 Sam Snead became the first golfer to break 60 in 18 holes in a major tournament. Do you ever dream of breaking a record? What record-breaking activity would you like to achieve?

May 17

British surgeon Edward Jenner was born on May 17, 1749. Create an epitaph that expresses his contribution to society.

68

May 18

On May 18, 1980, volcanic activity began in Mount St. Helens in the Cascade Mountains of Washington. About 60 people would die as a result of the eruption that would last until June 12. One of those people was 84-year-old Harry S. Truman, who refused to leave his home of 50 years. Choose a point of view. Then write a letter to Mr. Truman trying to convince him to leave or to the authorities to convince them that Mr. Truman is right to stay.

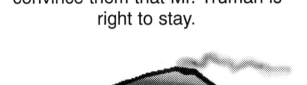

May 19

On May 19–20, 1928, a frog-jumping contest was held at Angels Camp, Calaveras County, California. It has become an annual event. It commemorates Mark Twain's famous story, "The Celebrated Jumping Frog of Calaveras County." Invent a funny contest.

May 20

On this date in 1862 President Lincoln approved the Homestead Act, which had been passed by both houses of Congress the day before. Explain the provisions of that law.

May 21

On this date in 1881 the American Red Cross was organized by Clara Barton. In 1882 it became part of the International Red Cross. Judge the importance of this organization. Create a poster showing one of the ways it helps.

69

May 22

Mary Cassatt was born on May 22, 1844. Although born in Pennsylvania, she spent much of her time in Europe. Influenced greatly by Edgar Degas, she exhibited her paintings with the Impressionists. She also urged her wealthy friends and relatives to purchase Impressionist paintings, thus increasing their popularity in America. In her honor create a word search of famous artists.

May 23

Carolus Linneus was born in Sweden on May 23, 1707. Botanist and explorer, he created a uniform system of naming plants and animals. In his honor choose a plant or animal and classify it giving its class, order, genus, and species.

May 24

On May 24, 1844, Samuel Morse sent a message marking the opening of the first commercial telegraph line in the United States. It went from Baltimore, MD, to Washington, D.C. Find out what the message was. Write it in Morse Code, the system of dots and dashes developed by Morse. Use a single slash (/) to separate letters and a double slash (//) to separate words.

May 25

On May 25, 1803, Ralph Waldo Emerson was born in Boston, Massachusetts. He was a poet, essayist, and lecturer. Emerson became the principal spokesperson for the group of New England writers and philosophers known as Transcendentalists. Find out the basic belief of the Transcendentalists.

May 26

Sally Kristen Ride was born on May 26, 1951, in Stanford, CA. She almost became a professional tennis player, but she decided to pursue a career in physics instead. In 1978 she received a doctorate in astrophysics. For what is Sally Ride best known?

May 27

The Golden Gate Bridge in California opened on May 27, 1937. Until the completion of the Verrazano-Narrows Bridge in 1964, it remained the longest suspension bridge in the world. Define "suspension bridge." Name other types of bridges.

May 28

British author Ian Fleming was born on May 28, 1908. Write a poem about his most famous literary character.

May 29

Ebenezer Butterick, the inventor of standardized paper patterns for clothing, was born in Massachusetts on May 29, 1826. Create an ad to promote the sale of Butterick's new patterns.

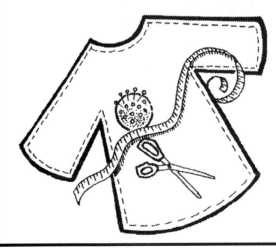

May 30

On May 30, 1848, William G. Young of Baltimore, MD, received a patent for an ice cream freezer.
In his honor invent a new flavor of ice cream.

May 31

American poet Walt Whitman was born on May 31, 1819. His poems exalted the common man and American individualism. One of his themes was the Civil War. Write a poem about the Civil War.

June 1

The first book fair was held in New York City on June 1, 1802. Plan a book fair for primary grade children. What books would you include?

June 2

[Henry] Lou Gehrig died on June 2, 1941, of amyotrophic lateral sclerosis. Write an acrostic poem about him.

72

June 3

African-American surgeon Charles Drew was born on June 3, 1904. Draw a picture that shows Drew's greatest contribution.

June 4

George III of Great Britain was born on June 4, 1738. He reigned as king of Great Britain and Ireland from 1760 to 1820. Compose three questions you would like to ask King George III.

June 5

Anthropologist Ruth Benedict was born on June 5, 1887. She is best known for her work *Patterns of Culture*. In her honor research a culture you know little about. Write five facts about that culture.

June 6

This date in 1944 was D-Day. Find out what this means.

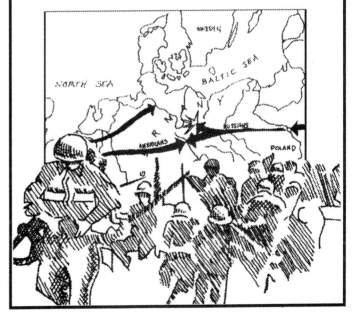

73

June 7

The first laboratory devoted exclusively to microbiology was dedicated on June 7, 1954. It was part of Rutgers University in New Jersey. The first director of the institute was Dr. Selman Abraham Waksman. In 1952 Dr. Waksman had won the Nobel Prize for Medicine or Physiology. Create a headline for a newspaper that explains why he won.

June 8

Renowned American architect Frank Lloyd Wright was born on June 8, 1867. In his honor design your "dream house." Draw a floor plan of the inside of the house.

June 9

Archaeologist Howard Carter was born on May 9, 1873. He made one of the most important contributions to Egyptology. Design a poster advertising a museum exhibit of his findings.

June 10

Singer and actress Judy Garland was born on June 10, 1922. The daughter of vaudeville performers, she made her stage debut when only three years old! She appeared in many films, but one in particular bought her international stardom. It was based on a novel by L. Frank Baum. Design a broadside featuring this film.

74

June 11

Today is Kamehameha Day in Hawaii. Find out who Kamehameha was and why he is honored.

June 12

Swiss author Johanna Spyri was born on June 12, 1829. Her novel *Heidi* has brought enjoyment to young readers for generations. Read *Heidi.* Tell why you think it has such enduring appeal.

June 13

The June 13, 1966, decision in the case of Miranda *v.* Arizona had a profound impact on the rights of citizens held in police custody. Explain.

June 14

Today is Flag Day. The American flag was adopted on this date in 1777. Create a couplet about the flag.

75

June 15

One June 15, 1752, Benjamin Franklin demonstrated the relationship between lightning and electricity. Thunder and lightning are the result of static electricity. Explain.

June 16

On June 16, 1933, President Franklin Delano Roosevelt authorized the Public Works Administration. Its purpose was to reduce unemployment and increase purchasing power through the construction of highways and public buildings. In 1939 the WPA was slowly dissolved. Guess why it was no longer needed.

June 17

One June 17, 1950, the first kidney transplant from one human to another was successfully performed by Dr. Richard Lawler. Prepare a radio or TV spot asking people to consider organ donations.

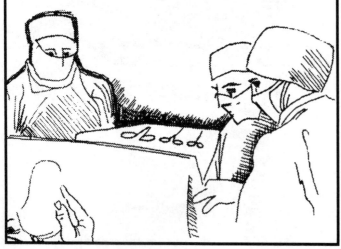

June 18

Did you ever hear the expression "to meet one's waterloo"? Find out what happened at Waterloo, Belgium, on June 18, 1815. Use your information to explain the meaning of the phrase.

76

June 19

The first woman to fly entirely around the world as a passenger on a heavier-than-air plane was Marjorie Shuler. She began her trip from Southampton, England, on June 4, 1939. She went from Europe to Africa, across Asia, to Australia, to Bangkok, to Hong Kong, across the Pacific to San Francisco, to New York, and across the Atlantic to Marseilles. Plan a trip around the world. Where will you stop?

June 20

The Great Seal of the United States Government was adopted on June 20, 1782. The eagle represents strength; the olive branch, peace; and the 13 arrows, the 13 states—ready for war if necessary. Design a seal for your class.

June 21

Depending on the year, June 21 or 22 marks the summer solstice in the Northern Hemisphere, where it is the longest day of the year. Create a cartoon that shows the length of the day in the Arctic Circle.

June 22

German author Erich Maria Remarque was born on June 22, 1898. He is best known for his novel *All Quiet on the Western Front*. It tells the horrors of the war from the point of view of its 19-year-old hero. Find out which war was the focus of the book.

77

June 23

U.S. running great Wilma Rudolph was born on June 23, 1940. She overcame crippling childhood illnesses to become one of the greatest sprinters of all time. In fact, she was the first American woman to earn three track-and-field gold medals at one Olympics. She died on November 12, 1994. Write about someone who overcame adversity to achieve success.

June 24

One June 24, 1807, Aaron Burr was indicted for treason; however, he was found not guilty of an "overt act" of treason. Find out what treasonous plan Burr was suspected of plotting. As the prosecutor in his trial, write your opening statement.

June 25

George Armstrong Custer is best known for his "last stand" at the Battle of Little Bighorn. He and all 266 of his men were killed by the Sioux. Many accused Custer of having been too rash. In spite of the fact that people remember him for leading his men into a massacre, Custer had distinguished himself earlier in his life. Create an epitaph for him that honors a great accomplishment.

June 26

The Virginia Company held a lottery as far back as June 26, 1614. The prize was 4,500 crowns. (A crown was a British coin.) Suppose you won a lottery worth a million dollars. How would you spend the money?

$$$$$$$$$$$$$$$$$$$$$$$$$$$$$$$$

PICK 6 LOTTO

A. 03 07 14 17 29 33
B. 01 05 18 23 26 31

···· Grand Prize ····
···· ONE MILLION DOLLARS

78

June 27

The first legislation regarding seat belts in automobiles was enacted on June 27, 1955. Create a poster encouraging people to wear seat belts.

June 28

On this date in 1968 a law was enacted that established Monday observances of five federal holidays: Washington's Birthday, Memorial Day, Labor Day, Columbus Day, and Veterans Day. Choose a point of view. Write a letter to the editor telling why you think this was or was not a good idea.

June 29

French aviator and writer Antoine Saint-Exupéry was born on June 29, 1900. His book *Le Petit Prince*, or *The Little Prince*, was published in 1944. Although enjoyed by children, it was really meant for adults. Read *The Little Prince*. Create a design for a sampler using the moral of the story.

June 30

The 20th Amendment was enacted on June 30, 1971. What was the provision of this amendment?

79

Daily Activities for July and August

An activity is given for each day of July and August. Use them as homework assignments, extra credit, daily openers, and so on. Background information is provided in the Answer Section as necessary.

JULY 1—On this date in 1731 the first circulating library was organized. Find out who organized it and where.

JULY 2—July 2, 1964, President Lyndon B. Johnson signed an important bill. What was it?

JULY 3—On July 3, 1754, the first battle of the French and Indian War was fought at Fort Necessity, PA. Who was involved in this battle? Who won?

JULY 4—On July 4, 1848, the cornerstone was laid for a national monument to George Washington. Draw a picture of that monument.

JULY 5—Phineas T. Barnum was born on July 5, 1810. Draw a picture advertising The Greatest Show on Earth.

JULY 6—On this date in 1945 the Medal of Freedom was established by President Truman. Write a dictionary entry explaining what it is.

JULY 7—Artist Marc Chagall was born on July 7, 1887. Among his recurring motifs were roof-top violinists and floating bridges. Many of his dreamlike paintings were based on personal experiences. Paint a picture based on an experience in your life.

JULY 8—On July 8, 1776, the Declaration of Independence was read publicly. Do a Readers' Theater performance reenacting the event.

JULY 9—On July 9, 1872, the doughnut cutter was patented. Today doughnut "holes" are sold as tiny doughnut balls. Draw a picture of something else that might be done with the "holes."

JULY 10—Artist James Whistler was born on this date in 1834. His painting of a relative became famous. Which relative?

JULY 11—E.B. White was born on July 11, 1819. Create a jacket cover for one of his children's books.

JULY 12—On July 12, 1882, the first ocean pier was completed in Atlantic City, New Jersey. Propose an attraction for the pier.

JULY 13—Actor Harrison Ford was born on July 13, 1942. In *Indiana Jones* he played the role of an archaeologist. Explain what archaeology is and the role of an archaeologist.

JULY 14—July 14, Bastille Day, is a national holiday in France. What does it commemorate?

JULY 15—Rembrandt was born on July 15, 1606. In his honor create a word search puzzle of famous artists.

JULY 16—July 16, 1941, marked the end of baseball player Joe Di Maggio's hitting streak. Design an award that shows what record he broke.

JULY 17—On July 17, 1975, *Apollo XVIII* docked with *Soyuz XIX.* Why was this special?

JULY 18—On July 18, 1940, Igor Sikorsky made the first successful flight in a certain kind of aircraft. Draw a picture of that type of aircraft.

JULY 19—On July 19, 1969, John Fairfax arrived at the beach in Hollywood, Florida. He had made the 180-day, solo, transatlantic trip from Las Palmas, Canary Islands, in a rowboat! As his mother, write him a letter to arrive *before* he sets out on his trip.

JULY 20—On July 20, 1969, Neil Armstrong and Edwin Aldrin, Jr., landed on the moon. Michael Collins remained in the Command Module. Compare and contrast their journey to the one made by John Fairfax which ended the previous day.

JULY 21—On July 21, 1861, the Battle of Bull Run Creek was fought in Virginia. It was the first serious engagement of the Civil War. Write a newspaper headline showing the outcome.

JULY 22—Austrian botanist Gregor Johann Mendel was born on July 22, 1822. For what is he best known?

JULY 23—On July 23, 1829, William Burt of Michigan received a patent for his "typographer." It was the first typewriter. Suppose Mr. Burt travelled magically through time to the present. Write a soliloquy for him upon witnessing modern personal computers.

JULY 24—Simón Bolívar was born in Caracas, Venezuela, on July 24, 1783. Explain why he is called The Great Liberator.

JULY 25—American artist Thomas Eakins was born on July 25, 1844. He is best known for his realistic portraits of friends and relatives. Another favorite subject was outdoor sports. Paint or draw a picture using one of these motifs.

JULY 26—The first book on Esperanto was published on July 26, 1887. What is Esperanto?

JULY 27—Ice skater Peggy Fleming was born on July 27, 1948. She won the only U.S. gold medal in ice skating at the 1968 Olympic Games. As Peggy Fleming, write an entry in your diary describing how you felt while receiving your medal.

JULY 28—On July 28, 1933, the first singing telegram was delivered by Western Union. From 1950 on these telegrams have been delivered by phone. Create a singing telegram you might send to someone.

JULY 29—On July 29, 1958, NASA was organized. NASA is an acronym. What do the letters stand for?

JULY 30—On July 30, 1898, the first automobile advertisement was published in the *Scientific American*. Its advertisement of the Winton Motor Car Co., Cleveland, Ohio, appeared under the caption "Dispense with a Horse." Think of another caption for the ad.

JULY 31—The first patent granted by the U.S. government was made on July 31, 1790. Think of something you would like to invent.

AUGUST 1—Shredded Wheat Biscuits were patented on this date in 1893. Suppose you were having a special guest for breakfast. Think of something original you could serve.

AUGUST 2—James "Wild Bill" Hickok was killed on August 2, 1876, while playing poker. Research his life and write a clerihew about him.

AUGUST 3—On August 3, 1958, the first underwater crossing of the North Pole was made by the *Nautilus*, an atomic-powered submarine. It was under the command of William Anderson. Do you think you would have enjoyed being part of that crew? Explain.

AUGUST 4—Swedish diplomat Raoul Gustaf Wallenberg was born on August 4, 1912. Find out why the U.S. Congress made him an honorary citizen in 1981. Only one other person was so honored. Do you know who that was?

AUGUST 5—On August 5, 1861, the first federal income tax law was enacted. Guess why.

AUGUST 6—Comedienne Lucille Ball was born on August 6, 1911. She is best known for the situation comedy *I Love Lucy*. In her honor, create a new episode for the series. Describe in detail what happens.

AUGUST 7—On this date in 1869 Charles Pickering took the first photograph of a total solar eclipse. Draw a diagram that explains a solar eclipse.

AUGUST 8—On August 8, 1974, President Richard Nixon became the first U.S. President to resign. Who was then appointed President?

AUGUST 9—On August 9, 1939, Jesse Owens became the first American athlete to win 4 medals at the Olympic Games. In what venue did he win?

AUGUST 10—Anges Gonxha Bojazhiu, better known as Mother Teresa, was born in Yugoslavia on August 10, 1910. In 1979 she was awarded the Nobel Peace Prize. Judge the selection of Mother Teresa for this great honor.

AUGUST 11—Author Alex Haley was born on August 11, 1921. He is best known for his book *Roots: The Saga of an American Family*. An acclaimed TV miniseries was based on it. Write a story about your grandparents or other ancestors.

AUGUST 12—American educator and poet Katherine Lee Bates was born on August 12, 1859. For what is she best known?

AUGUST 13—Alfred Hitchcock was born in England on August 13, 1899. He is best known for his suspense stories with surprising twists. In his honor create a plot for a mystery. Your plot should have a twist, or unexpected change.

AUGUST 14—Queen Emma, widow of King Kamehameha IV, of the Sandwich Islands was the first queen to visit the U.S.A. She was received by President Johnson on August 14, 1866. What are the Sandwich Islands now called?

AUGUST 15—On this date in 1635 the first recorded hurricane hit the U.S., ravaging Plimoth (Plymouth) Colony. Create a Scrambled Weather Terms game. For example, if "TOSMR" were given, the answer would be STORM. Exchange with classmates to solve.

AUGUST 16—On August 16, 1916, the U.S. and Great Britain signed the Migratory Bird Treaty. It was meant to protect migratory birds in the U.S. and Canada. Choose a migratory bird and map its migration route.

AUGUST 17—David "Davy" Crockett was born on August 17, 1786. Write a poem about him.

AUGUST 18—The 19th Amendment was approved on this date in 1920. What did it grant?

AUGUST 19—American humorous poet Ogden Nash was born on August 19, 1902. In his honor, write a funny couplet.

AUGUST 20—On August 20, 1964, the Office of Economic Opportunity was authorized by the Economic Opportunity Act of 1964. The act provided funds for vocational training, work-training camps, youth centers for poor areas, and loans to small businesses. President Lyndon Johnson said this was to fight a special kind of war. What did he call that war?

AUGUST 21—Hawaii became the 50th state on August 21, 1959. Hawaii is an archipelago. Explain. Name the major islands. Where do most of the people live?

AUGUST 22—Science-fiction writer Ray Bradbury was born on August 22, 1920. Write a definition of science fiction.

AUGUST 23—American poet Edgar Lee Masters, best known for his *Spoon River Anthology*, was born on August 23, 1869. Spoon River is a fictional small town. In his work former residents of Spoon River speak from the grave about their dreary lives in the small town. It is like a series of free-verse epitaphs. Write an epitaph for a fictional former resident of your town.

AUGUST 24—On August 24, 1869, a patent was issued for a waffle iron. Brainstorm and try to think of many different appliances we have today that did not exist in 1869.

AUGUST 25—On August 25, 1814, President Madison became the first U.S. President to face enemy gunfire while in office. Explain the circumstances.

AUGUST 26—The first successful public school kindergarten was authorized on August 26, 1873, by the St. Louis, Missouri, Board of Education. Evaluate the choice of the word "kindergarten."

AUGUST 27—Lyndon Baines Johnson was born on August 27, 1908. He became President on November 22, 1963. Describe the circumstances.

AUGUST 28—On August 28, 1938, the School of Speech of Northwestern University conferred an honorary degree on Charlie McCarthy. What was unusual about this?

AUGUST 29—On August 29, 1957, Senator Strom Thurmond's filibuster ended. Explain what is meant by a filibuster.

AUGUST 30—Author Mary Wollstonecraft Shelley was born on August 30, 1797, in London. For what work is she most famous?

AUGUST 31—Frank Robinson was born on August 31 1935. He was the first baseball player to win the "Most Valuable Player" award in both major leagues. in 1982 he was elected to the Baseball Hall of Fame. If you could be voted "most valuable" for something, what would you want that thing to be?

Answers and Background Information

Background information and answers are given as appropriate. Many activities call for original, creative answers. Answers are not given for those.

September

Sept. 1:   The 13th Amendment abolished slavery.

Sept. 2:   Eugene Field wrote "Wynken, Blynken, and Nod" and "Little Boy Blue."

Sept. 3:   Sullivan was one of the first to design a skyscraper with iron frames and straight lines. He's credited with inventing the skyscraper.

Sept. 4:   George Eastman received a patent for his "Kodak" roll camera.

Sept. 5:   Georgia did not send representatives.

Sept. 6:   President McKinley was assassinated in Buffalo, New York, while attending the Pan-American Exposition.

Sept. 10:   This secured the Northwest for the United States during the War of 1812.

Sept. 12:   They discovered a prehistoric cave magnificently decorated with engraved, drawn, and painted animals. The cave is believed to have served as a center for the performance of hunting and magical rites.

Sept. 14:   Sharecropping, or tenant farming, was a system of agricultural organization. The landowners contributed land; the tenants contributed labor. Each contributed varying amounts of capital and management. Payment to the landowners were in the form of a share of the crop, cash, or combination of both. Sharecropping became the accepted labor system throughout the South during the Reconstruction Period. The planters preferred it because they didn't have to pay wages. Without land or money, most freedmen had to continue working for their former masters. Now, however, they could live in individual cabins on tracts of land they rented. Sharecroppers found it very difficult to get out of debt; therefore, they were virtually bound to the soil, for the law prohibited them from leaving unless all their bills were paid. The South, however, was extremely poor during Reconstruction, and some bad crop years in the late 1860s followed by a general agricultural depression of the 1870s made matters worse.

Sept. 16:   The *Mayflower* left Plymouth, England, with 102 passengers, including 32 children. There were 2 dogs and 25 crew members also on board. Rough seas and storms made their two-and-a-half-month journey in cramped conditions difficult to bear. The rough seas also kept them from reaching their planned destination, Virginia. Instead they landed at Provincetown, Massachusetts.

Sept. 17:   Baron von Stuben helped train the troops at Valley Forge.

Sept. 18:   Among the facts that might be included are the following: Washington was born on April 5, 1856, in Franklin County, Virginia. He was born in a slave hut. After emancipation, his family moved to West Virginia. As a child he worked in a salt furnace and a coal mine. He wanted an education; therefore, he got a job as a janitor to help pay expenses while attending the Hampton Normal and Agricultural Institute in Virginia. He returned to West Virginia and taught children at a day school and adults at night. He studied at Wayland Seminary in Washington, D.C., from 1878–79. In 1881, he headed the newly established Normal School for Blacks in Tuskegee. He became the institute's main developer. When he died on December 14, 1915, there were more than 100 buildings. Washington was the most influential spokesman for blacks between 1895 and 1915.

Sept. 19:   *Steamboat Willie* was the first cartoon to use sound.

Sept. 20:   Fiorello La Guardia was a U.S. Congressman and 3-term mayor of New York City (1933–35). He became known as the "Little Flower." La Guardia fought corruption, fostered civic improvement, and was pro-labor. He had a real flair for the dramatic. Once he assigned Jewish police officers to escort a visiting Nazi delegation. Another time he shut off the heat in the room where labor negotiations were being held to try to end a coal strike. He was also known for reading the Sunday comics over the radio to keep up morale.

Sept. 21:   In 1673, Louis Joliet and Father Marquette traveled by canoe from Green Bay along the Fox, Wisconsin, and Mississippi Rivers. When they got to the mouth of the Arkansas River, they returned. They were certain that the Mississippi emptied into the Gulf of Mexico, not the Gulf of California as previously believed.

Sept. 23:   He said, "I have not yet begun to fight."

Sept. 26:   In March 1775, Daniel Boone and 28 others were hired to blaze a trail through the Cumberland Gap, a notch in the juncture of Virginia, Tennessee, and Kentucky. In spite of Indian attacks, they built the

Wilderness Road. It ran from eastern Virginia to the interior of Kentucky. The road became the main route to the West. It made possible the opening of the first settlements in Kentucky.

Sept. 27: A caricature is a pictorial representation in which the subject's distinctive features or peculiarities are deliberately distorted or exaggerated.

Sept. 30: Roger Maris broke Babe Ruth's record in 1961. Both Ruth and Maris played for the New York Yankees.

October

Oct. 2: Nat Turner was a slave who believed he had been called upon by God to lead his people out of bondage. On August 21, 1831, with the help of seven fellow slaves, he murdered his owner and his owner's family. He then headed towards the county seat, Jerusalem, Virginia, hoping to capture the armory there. In two days he and his followers murdered 51 white people. Although he had expected greater support, however, only 75 had rallied to his cause. The state militia and its force of 3,000 men easily put down the insurrection. Turner was caught, tried, and hanged. His rebellion, however, put an end to the idea that slaves were incapable of mounting an armed revolt.

Oct. 3: Black Hawk, a leader of a faction of Sauk and Fox, defied U.S. government orders to leave the fertile fields of his village (Sautenuk, now part of Rockford, Illinois). The result was the short, tragic Black Hawk War. In 1832 Black Hawk and his followers returned to the disputed land, hoping to plant crops. He also hoped for some help from other tribes and possibly the British—that help never came. Black Horse was forced to retreat into Wisconsin. On August 2, the Battle of Bad Axe River took place. Black Horse stood no chance against the Illinois militia, which was reinforced by U.S. troops. Only about 150 of the Indians—including women and children—survived. What's more, the spirit of the Native Americans in the region had been broken by the massacre. They virtually abandoned all of the Northwest Territory.

Oct. 4: Answers will vary but should include that he was a painter, illustrator, and sculptor known for realistic portrayals of the American West. He specialized in depicting Native Americans, cowboys, horses, and other aspects of life on the Plains.

Oct. 5: Tecumseh advocated resistance against encroaching white settlement. He tried to encourage the tribes to stop fighting amongst themselves and to unite in an intertribal alliance.

Oct. 12: The gyrocompass is driven by electricity and is, therefore, unaffected by iron or steel and its axis always points true north.

Oct. 13: Mary McCauley is better known as Molly Pitcher. Her husband was an artilleryman at the Battle of Monmouth. She brought water to the men. When her husband collapsed, she replaced him at the cannon and fought the rest of the battle.

Oct. 14: The plan of government was very liberal. It included the principle of religious freedom and also contained many reforms in the penal code. For example, it eliminated the death penalty for many crimes that called for capital punishment under English law.

Oct. 16: John Brown was a militant white abolitionist who believed the Lord had chosen him to destroy slave owners. On October 16, 1859, he attacked the U.S. army at Harpers Ferry, Virginia. His plan was to use the guns and ammunition to arm the slaves in Virginia. Although he was captured and hanged before he could put his plan into effect, he became a martyr for other abolitionists and blacks. To the slave owners he was a madman who tried to arouse the slaves to murder their masters; he frightened them greatly.

Oct. 17: Burgoyne's defeat at Saratoga raised the morale of the Patriot troops. It also showed foreign nations that Americans had a chance to win the war. It made it easier to convince France, Spain, and Holland to support the colonies.

Oct. 18: United States Secretary of State William F. Seward persuaded Congress to purchase the land now called Alaska from Russia for $7,200,000.00. Even though the cost was only a few cents an acre, many were against the purchase. They called the purchase "Seward's Folly." The formal transfer of ownership took place on October 18, 1867, at Sitka.

Oct. 19: Lafayette had done a great deal to obtain French aid for the Americans. As General Washington marched to Yorktown he was met by French troops sent to assist him. Also, the French navy blockaded Yorktown by sea; this prevented British reinforcements and supplies from getting through.

Oct. 21: Alfred Nobel was a great philanthropist. The terms of his will specified that the bulk of his fortune be held in trust for the establishment of international awards. Awarded annually since 1901 in physics, chemistry, physiology or medicine, and peace, these Nobel Prizes came to be the most prestigious of all international awards. Some may think Nobel wanted to ease his conscience about the explosives.

Oct. 22: He refused to swear allegiance to the Confederacy.

86

Oct. 24: A compound microscope is one with two or more lenses. The eyepiece is one of the lenses. Light usually travels in a straight line. When light passes through the objective lens of a microscope, it refracts, or changes direction. It is this refraction that causes the image to be upside down and backwards.

November

Nov. 2: Women were allowed to vote for the first time in a presidential election.

Nov. 4: Will Rogers had Native American ancestors. In fact, he was born in Ooologoh, Indian Territory, which later became the state of Oklahoma.

Nov. 5: Andrew Hamilton, a brilliant Philadelphia lawyer, defended Zenger. He argued that the statements printed in the articles were true. The jury acquitted Zenger on the grounds that his charges against the governor were based on fact and, therefore, not libelous. This became the key consideration in libel cases from then on.

Nov. 6: John Philip Sousa was called the March King. He composed about 140 military marches, the most famous of which is *The Stars and Stripes Forever,* composed in 1897.

Nov. 7: May 14, 1804, the 3 ships started up the Missouri River. By November they had made the difficult journey up the Missouri through what is now Missouri, Kansas, Iowa, Nebraska, and South Dakota to what is now North Dakota, where they wintered. In the spring they headed west to what is now Montana. When they reached the Great Falls of the Missouri, they built crude wagons to carry the canoes and baggage around it. Still in Montana, they got horses and went on horseback over the Continental Divide to the headwaters of the Clearwater River. They built canoes, which they used to travel down the Clearwater River to the Snake River and then to the mouth of the Columbia River, which flowed westward to the Pacific Ocean. On November 7 they sighted the Pacific. On November 15 they reached the mouth of the Columbia River. They built Fort Clatsop and spent the winter on the Pacific Coast. In March 1806 they began their return trip.

Nov. 9: Benjamin Banneker built the first clock in America. He was a surveyor and worked for Pierre L'Enfant, city planner for the city of Washington. When L'Enfant was dismissed, Banneker reproduced and carried out his plans. He published an annual almanac for the years 1792–1802. He was a gifted astronomer and mathematician and predicted the solar eclipse of 1789.

Nov. 10: Hiawatha was a legendary chief of the Onondagas. He is said to have lived in the mid-1400s. Indian tradition credits him with the formation of the League of Five Nations, known as the Iroquois League. The story of the formation of the League is part myth. Before the League there was much fighting amongst the Iroquois nations. Legend tells us that among those who proposed a council of peace was Hiawatha. A Huron named Deganawidah (probably mythical) told of a vision he had had in which a great spruce tree with five roots reached the sky. The soil in which it was rooted was composed of righteousness and peace. Atop the tree was an eagle. Deganawidah, called Peacemaker by the Iroquois, interpreted his vision as a call from Teharonhiawagon, the Master of Life, to unite. Hiawatha traveled with Peacemaker to convince the Iroquois to join the federation. All were convinced except the Onondagas, who had living among them the wicked Odorarhoh (Atoharho), who had killed Hiawatha's family. Hiawatha put aside personal feelings and went with Peacemaker and convinced Odorarhoh to change his ways. According to some versions of the legend, Odorarhoh had snakes in his hair and Hiawatha combed the snakes (evil thoughts) from his hair. The League united the Mohawk, Oneida, Onondago, Cayuga, and Seneca. (In 1722 the Tuscarora also joined.)

Nov. 12: In 1848 Elizabeth Cady Stanton circulated petitions to encourage passage of a New York statute giving property rights to married women. With Lucretia Mott, she led the first women's right convention in the United States. It was held in Seneca Falls, NY, and Rochester, NY. All of the resolutions she had drawn were adopted, including the resolution favoring suffrage, which was opposed by Mrs. Mott. In 1850, she began a long association with another suffragist, Susan B. Anthony. In 1863 the Women's National Loyal League was formed. Elizabeth Stanton was its president and Susan B. Anthony was its secretary. The aim of the league was to gather signatures on petitions asking Congress to pass an amendment abolishing slavery.

Nov. 13: General T.J. "Stonewall" Jackson was fatally wounded.

Nov. 14: Robert Fulton was an inventor and artist. Although he did not invent the steamboat, he did design the first serviceable steamboat. The *Clermont* made her first voyage up the Hudson River to Albany on August 7, 1807. It was soon used regularly by paying customers who traveled between New York and Albany.

Nov. 15: Congress could pass laws, but it couldn't enforce them. Each state could decide whether or not to accept the laws. Congress could declare war, but it couldn't tax the states to pay for the armies. It could ask for money, but no more. Congress could make treaties with foreign nations, but it had no power to make the states honor those treaties. Congress could not control interstate trade or trade between states and other countries. Also, Congress didn't control the money, as each state could issue its own currency.

Nov. 16: Some possibilities are breads, muffins, tortillas, hominy grits, polenta, popcorn, cereals, and scrapple; livestock feed; and oil for cooking. Husks can be used to make dolls. Cobs were used for fuel and to make corncob pipes.

Nov. 17: Answers will vary, but students might be interested in knowing what Benjamin Franklin thought of the choice. The following is an excerpt from a letter he wrote on January 26, 1784: "I wish the bald eagle had not been chosen as the representative of our country; he is a bird of bad moral character; like those among us who live by sharping and robbing, he is generally poor, and often very lousy. The turkey is a much more respectable bird, and withal a true original native of America."

Nov. 19: Answers will vary, but especially memorable was Lincoln's definition of democracy as a "government of the people, by the people, and for the people."

Nov. 21: The Mayflower Compact was drawn up to ensure that people wouldn't go off and settle on their own. It bound the people together by pledging them to abide by any laws and regulations that might later be established. The Mayflower Compact was not a constitution, but it did contain the seeds for a democratic society. It provided for the popular elections of leaders (John Carver was elected governor shortly after the signing.) It also provided for citizen participation in local affairs. (An outgrowth of this would be the town meeting, common in New England.) In general, the Mayflower Compact was the foundation of government in Plymouth Colony.

Nov. 23: Students might include the following books: *The Gremlins, James and the Giant Peach, Charlie and the Chocolate Factory, Chitty Chitty Bang Bang,* and *The Great Glass Elevator.*

Nov. 24: Zachary Taylor was called Old Rough and Ready. He had been elected on the Whig ticket as a hero of the Mexican War.

Nov. 26: President Washington proclaimed it a day of general thanksgiving for the adoption of the Constitution.

Nov. 28: *Mariner 4* was the first satellite to transmit a close-up photograph of Mars.

Nov. 30: Mark Twain was the riverman's term for water that was just barely safe for navigation. Clemens probably thought it appropriate for the ridiculous tall tales he had been telling so convincingly that people actually believed them.

December

Dec. 2: There would be no further European colonization in the New World. The U.S. would abstain from European political affairs. European nations would not intervene in the governments of the Western Hemisphere.

Dec. 3: He performed the first human heart transplant. The patient lived for 18 days.

Dec. 4: He was an American general who had resisted British invasions into the South during the Revolutionary War. In March 1776 he took command of a fort he had built of sand and logs on Sullivan's Island, which is off Charleston. He held the fort against heavy British attack. The fort was then named in his honor.

Dec. 5: This amendment repealed the 18th amendment, which forbade the sale of alcoholic beverages in the United States.

Dec. 6: A cinquain is a 5-lined poem. Although the lines do not have to rhyme, they do have a set pattern. Line 1 has a 2-syllable noun. Line 2 had one or more adjectives with a total of 4 syllables. Line 3 has verbs (-ing forms work well) with a total of 6 syllables. Line 4 has 8 syllables and tells how you feel about the noun. Line 5 has a 2-syllable noun that makes you think of the first noun.

Dec. 7: Japanese naval and air forces attacked American ships at Pearl Harbor, Hawaii. This attack brought the United States into World War II.

Dec. 8: In 1801 he showed that interchangeable parts for muskets could be mass produced. This made it possible to quickly repair many muskets.

Dec. 10: Since 1901 Nobel prizes have been awarded on December 10 in the areas of physics, chemistry, physiology or medicine, literature, and peace. Money is awarded under the terms of the will of Alfred Nobel, who died on this date in 1896.

Dec. 11: He abdicated the throne so he could marry Wallis Warfield Simpson, an American divorcee.

Dec. 12: Alexander Hamilton, James Madison, and John Jay each wrote newspaper essays in defense of the new governmental structure. They used the joint pseudonym "Publius." The essays were intended to encourage ratification of the Constitution and were later published in book form as *The Federalist*.

Dec. 13:   Menuhin was born on April 22, 1916. His violin performance of Mendelsohn's *Violin Concerto* at age 7 caused a sensation. He was only 10 when he debuted at Carnegie Hall. A child prodigy is one who has exceptional talent at a young age.

Dec. 19:   President Eisenhower's message ended with the following: "...to all mankind, America's wish for peace on earth and good will toward men everywhere."

Dec. 20:   South Carolina announced that it was seceding from the United States. Mississippi, Florida, Alabama, Georgia, Louisiana, and Texas soon followed South Carolina's lead.

Dec. 22:   Some of Potter's tales include the following: *The Tale of Peter Rabbit, The Tailor of Gloucester, The Tale of Squirrel Nutkin, The Tale of Benjamin Bunny,* and *Mr. Jeremy Fisher.*

Dec. 23:   The Rosetta Stone was discovered in 1799 near the town of Rosetta (Rashid), Egypt. The inscriptions on the stone were in Egyptian hieroglyphic, demotic (a cursive form of Egyptian hieroglyphics), and Greek. Deciphering the inscriptions led to the understanding of hieroglyphic writing. English physicist Thomas Young and Jean-François Champollion are credited with the decipherment of the Rosetta Stone.

Dec. 24:   On December 24, 1814, a treaty was signed at Ghent, Belgium; however, news traveled slowly and news of the treaty hadn't yet arrived in America. The War of 1812 was already over when the Battle of New Orleans was fought.

Dec. 25:   At the outbreak of the Civil War she organized an agency to obtain and distribute supplies for the relief of wounded soldiers. She had obtained special permission from the Surgeon of the United States Army to "go on the sick transports in any direction." She followed the army as best she could—at first by wagon and then by railroad boxcar.

Dec. 26:   The day after Christmas came to be known as Boxing Day from the boxed gifts that were given to mail carriers, garbage collectors, and others who serve the community throughout the year. Today monetary gifts are often substituted for the boxed gifts.

Dec. 27:   Kepler discovered that the Earth and other planets travel in elliptical orbits around the sun.

Dec. 29:   To *impeach* means to accuse an official of misconduct in office and to bring him to trial. If the impeachment proceedings lead to a conviction, the official can be removed from office. It is the only legal way to force the President out of office. Certain procedures must be followed as per the Constitution. Members of the House of Representatives must vote to charge the President with a crime. The President would then be brought to trial before the Senate, which would act as jury. The Chief Justice of the Supreme Court would preside over the trial. Two-thirds of the Senate must find the President guilty for a conviction.

Dec. 31:   Roberto Clemente died in an airplane crash. He had been leading an effort in Puerto Rico to aid the victims of a violent earthquake in Nicaragua. The cargo plane in which he was flying crashed after takeoff from San Juan.

January

Jan 1:   Both freed slaves; however, the Emancipation Proclamation applied only to slaves in the secessionist Southern states. It did not apply to those loyal slave states nor to those in federally occupied areas of the Confederacy. If the Thirteenth Amendment had not been passed, even those freed under the Emancipation Proclamation could have been re-enslaved after the war was over.

Jan 2:   Nathaniel Bacon was a planter with two estates in Virginia. He led a group of settlers who, like himself, believed in unlimited expansion. In 1676 he led an expedition against the Indians. When the Governor of Virginia, William Berkeley, denounced their activities and called the activity "Bacon's Rebellion," Bacon's men attacked Berkeley and took control of most of Virginia Colony. Bacon died in October of that year, however, and the rebellion collapsed.

Jan 4:   Louis Braille, who was accidentally blinded at the age of three, invented a system of writing to be used by blind persons. The modern system is a code of 63 characters, each made up of one to six dots arranged in a 6-position matrix. The characters are embossed into a page. To read, the blind person passes his or her fingers over the raised characters.

Jan 5:   "Our country!... may she always be in the right; but our country, right or wrong."

Jan 7:   Marian Anderson was the first African-American soloist to sing in the Metropolitan Opera.

Jan 8:   Elvis Presley was born on January 8, 1935.

Jan 9:   The Seeing Eye trains dogs to guide blind persons.

Jan 10: The Medal of Freedom is awarded to non-military persons "who contribute significantly to the quality of American life."

Jan 11: Alexander Hamilton, John Jay, and James Madison wrote a series of thoughtful newspaper articles. In these articles they explained how the new constitution worked and encouraged its ratification. The newspaper articles came to be known as *The Federalist*. Alexander Hamilton wrote more than 2/3 of the 85 articles.

Jan 13: His stories were about poor boys who rose from rags to riches. Their success was achieved by honesty, perseverance, hard work, and a touch of good luck.

Jan 14: Benedict Arnold's lavish spending and need for money to maintain his extravagant lifestyle probably motivated him to betray his country. He asked the British for a sum of 20,000 pounds if he could successfully surrender West Point to them. The mission failed; however, British contact Mayor John André was captured and hanged as a spy. Arnold escaped to Britain. In September 1781 he led a raid on New London, Connecticut, further antagonizing his former neighbors.

Jan 15: Matthew Brady is best known for his photographic record of the Civil War. He had invested about $100,000 in the project. Brady wrongly believed that the U.S. government would purchase his pictures after the war.

Jan 21: Some facts might include the following: He assisted French scientist Nicolles in surveying and mapping the upper Mississippi and Missouri Rivers in 1838. In 1841 he surveyed the Des Moines River. Then he mapped much of the Mississippi Valley and the Pacific Ocean. He surveyed the route west to Wyoming for the War Department. When emigration to the Oregon Territory increased, he thoroughly explored the Northwest and added a wealth of knowledge about the area's geography. He also crossed the Sierra Nevadas.

Jan 23: She received her M.D. degree from the Medical Institution of Geneva, New York (now the College of Medicine, Syracuse University). She became the first woman in America to earn a medical degree.

Jan 24: Maria Tallchief was a prima ballerina.

Jan 26: When he left the Philippines on March 11, 1942, General Douglas MacArthur said, "I shall return." He knew that Bataan, the last American stronghold, was about to fall to Japan. He made the other statements in a speech to Congress on April 19, 1951, a few days after President Truman removed him from command of the United Nations Forces (Korean War).

Jan 27: A portmanteau word is formed by combining sounds and meanings of two different words. Some examples are *brunch* (for breakfast and lunch), *chortle* (for chuckle and snort), and *smog* (for smoke and fog).

Jan 28: An acrostic is a poem or series of lines in which the first letter in each line forms a name, motto, or message. Facts will vary greatly, but may include the following: He was an English admiral. He was given a privateering commission from the Queen. He headed an expedition that circumnavigated the world. He was knighted by Queen Elizabeth. He commanded a fleet of 25 ships that set out to damage the Spanish Empire. He played an important role in the defeat of the Spanish Armada.

Jan 29: Paine believed that the colonists should do more than revolt against unfair taxation. He believed independence was necessary. Paine clearly expressed these views in a 50-page pamphlet "Common Sense." It was printed on January 10, 1776. More than 500,000 were sold in only a few months. This pamphlet was very influential in the ratification of the Declaration of Independence. On December 19, 1776, "The American Crisis: Number 1" was published. General Washington had it read to his troops at Valley Forge to boost their waning morale.

Jan 31: Both signed the Constitution for the state of New York.

February

Feb. 1: Harriet Tubman was an escaped slave who helped hundreds of other fugitive slaves escape via the Underground Railroad.

Feb. 2: Heifitz is known for the violin.

Feb. 3: Elizabeth Blackwell was the first woman to earn an M.D. degree from a medical school in the United States. She earned it from Geneva Medical College in New York in 1849.

Feb. 4: Blacks in Montgomery, Alabama, boycotted the buses for over a year. This marked the beginning of the civil rights movement in the United States.

Feb. 5: He hit 755 home runs. (In 1974 he hit his 715th, breaking Babe Ruth's record, which had stood since 1935.)

Feb. 6: He is called the "Sultan of Swat."

Feb. 7: Her books include *Little House in the Big Woods* (1932), *Farmer Boy* (1933), *Little House on the Prairie* (1935), *On the Banks of Plum Creek* (1937), *By the Shores of Silver Lake* (1939), *The Long Winter* (1940), and *These Happy Golden Years* (1943).

Feb. 10: The Treaty of Paris ended the conflict known as the French and Indian War. England and France fought for control of colonial North America. England was victorious. As a result of the treaty, France gave up all military and political power in North America.

Feb. 12: UMWA = United Mine Workers of America. AFL = American Federation of Labor. CIO = Congress of (originally for) Industrial Organization.

Feb. 15: Susan B. Anthony was a crusader for the women's suffrage movement and served as president of the National American Woman Suffrage Association from 1892–1900. The Nineteenth Amendment, ratified in 1920, gave women the right to vote.

Feb. 16: Esperanto is an artificial language with a vocabulary based on roots common to many European languages. There is also a regularized system of inflection. (Inflection is an alteration of a word form to indicate number, person, tense, or other grammatical features.) Esperanto was named for Dr. Esperanto, pseudonym for L.L. Zamenhof.

Feb. 18: Pluto was discovered on February 18, 1930.

Feb. 19: It was the first duel between ironclad men-of-war. The *Merrimack* had been built in the North, salvaged by the Confederates, and renamed the *Virginia*. The battle itself was indecisive, although most give the victory to the *Monitor.*

Feb. 20: On February 20, 1962, Glenn was blasted off in a capsule from Cape Canaveral, Florida. The bell-shaped capsule traveled around the Earth 3 times before it came down about 5 hours later. Glenn became the first American astronaut to orbit the Earth.

Feb. 22: The sonnet is a 14-lined lyric poem. The English sonnet is composed of 3 quatrains and a couplet with the following rhyme schemes: *abab, cdcd, efef,* and *gg.*

Feb. 25: It gave Congress the power "to lay and collect taxes on incomes, from whatever source derived..."

Feb. 26: A clerihew is a biographical, humorous quatrain. Usually the person is named in the first line of the poem.

Feb. 27: Francis Marion was known as the Swamp Fox. He earned the nickname during the Revolutionary War. General Marion led his men in surprise warfare. They made quick raids against the British and then disappeared into the swamps.

March

March 2: He tried to prevent the secession of Texas, but failed. When he refused to swear allegiance to the Confederacy, he was deposed.

March 4: Their nickname is the Fighting Irish.

March 5: It is called the Boston Massacre.

March 6: Each side wanted to control San Antonio. A force of less than 200 Texan volunteers tried to defend the Alamo against a Mexican force of 4,000 led by General Santa Anna. All of the Texans were killed, including Colonels William B. Travis and James Bowie and the legendary Davy Crockett. Six weeks later the Texans gained their independence as a result of General Sam Houston's victory at San Jacinto. Col. Sidney Sherman had rallied his volunteers at that battle with the battle cry "Remember the Alamo!"

March 8: He stated that "clear and present danger" was the only basis of curtailing the right of free speech. He used the following example: "The most stringent protection of free speech would not protect a man in falsely shouting 'fire' in a theater and causing a panic."

March 9: At Reykjavik, Iceland, in 1972, Fischer defeated then world champion Boris Spassky of the Soviet Union. In so doing he became the first American to hold the title of Chess Champion of the World.

March 10: A clerihew is a humorous biographical quatrain. The subject is usually named in the first line. It is named for its inventor, Edmund Clerihew Bentley (1875-1956).

March 11: Fleming discovered penicillin, which eventually would lead to the antibiotic therapy for infectious diseases. He shared the prize with Ernest Boris Chain and Howard Walter Florey. They further isolated, purified, and tested penicillin.

March 12: Boycott was the estate agent of the Earl of Erne in County Mayo, Ireland. The Land League was formed in 1879 when famine was a threat because of bad harvests. The league ordered landlords to lower rents. It also said that any landlord who took over the farm of an evicted tenant would be completely avoided

91

by supporters of the league. In 1880 Boycott, who was the estate agent of the Earl of Erne in County Mayo, refused to lower rents and tried to serve writs of eviction. Boycott and his family soon found themselves without servants, farmhands, mail delivery, and other services. The term "boycott" originated shortly after. At first it was used to describe any form of nonviolent intimidation. It later came to mean ostracism in business and social relations.

March 14: Relativity is "an approach to the study of time and space."

March 15: Julius Caesar was assassinated in the Senate on March 15, 44 B.C.

March 16: On July 20, 1969, Neil Armstrong and Edwin Aldrin landed on the moon in the lunar module *Eagle*. Michael Collins remained in the command module *Columbia*. Neil Armstrong became the first to set foot on the moon saying, "That's one small step for man, one giant leap for mankind."

March 17: Russian ballet dancer Rudolf Nureyev defected from the Soviet Union in 1961. He began dancing in America in 1962. Famed ballerina Margot Fonteyn was often his partner.

March 18: Grover Cleveland served from 1885–89 and 1893–97. He was the only U.S. President to serve two non-consecutive terms.

March 19: Lake Tanganyika is in East Africa between Zaire and Tanzania. It is the longest freshwater lake in the world (410 mi.or 660 km.) and the second deepest (4,710 ft. or 1,436 m.).

March 21: The instruments are harpsichord, violin, flute, and organ.

March 22: *Maser* is an acronym for microwave amplification by stimulated emission of radiation. *Laser* is an acronym for light amplification by stimulated emission of radiation.

March 23: Patrick Henry said it during a speech before the second Virginia Convention in Richmond.

March 24: On March 24, 1989, the *Exxon Valdez* tanker ran aground in Prince William Sound, Alaska. It spilled 200,00 barrels of crude oil. Thousands of animals were killed, including some very rare species. Bad weather and delays in the arrival of the necessary equipment hampered efforts to contain the spill.

March 25: Borglum is best known for the Mount Rushmore National Memorial in South Dakota. Using new methods, he carved the heads of Washington, Jefferson, Lincoln and T. Roosevelt.

March 26: On September 25, 1981, Sandra Day O'Connor was sworn in as an associate justice of the U.S. Supreme Court. She was the first woman to hold the position.

March 27: He won for the discovery of x-rays.

March 29: He was Vice President. He became President when William Henry Harrison died on April 4, 1841, only one month after taking office. He was the first Vice President to become President because of the death of the incumbent.

March 31: Cesar Chavez quit his job in the fields so that he could organize the Mexican-American farm workers. The workers had been very poorly paid. His work resulted in the first successful union of agricultural workers, the National Farm Workers Association. This association was the forerunner of the United Farm Workers of America. Chavez first became famous when he encouraged the grape pickers to strike in 1965. In 1668 he led a national boycott against California table grapes.

April

April 4: Dorothea Dix crusaded to improve conditions in prisons. She was especially concerned about the mentally ill, who were chained to chairs and integrated with vicious criminals. Because of her efforts, reforms were made both in the United States and abroad. Laws were passed that required the mentally ill to be placed in hospitals, not prisons.

April 5: The Joint Chiefs of Staff is the most important military advisory group of the United States. It is composed of the chiefs of the Army, Navy, and Air Force and sometimes the commandant of the Marines.

April 6: Four Eskimos and one African-American, Matthew Henson, accompanied Peary on his expedition. Some accounts say that Henson, Peary's assistant, actually reached the pole 45 minutes before Peary.

April 7: WHO is an acronym that stands for World Health Organization. It is part of the United Nations. Its three general purposes are to provide research services and to disseminate the information; to help control epidemic and endemic disease through vaccination programs, instruction regarding antibiotics and insecticides, assistance in setting up sanitation systems, and so on; and to assist the public health agencies of member nations.

April 8: With his 715th home run, Hank Aaron had broken the home-run record that had been held by Babe Ruth since 1935. Aaron finished his career with 755 home runs.

April 9: The Marquis de Lafayette was awarded citizenship first by Maryland and then by several other states.

April 10: Joseph Pulitzer became one of the most powerful and highly regarded journalists in the United States. His will provided for a series of awards to be given annually for outstanding public service in American journalism and letters. There are 8 prizes for journalism, 5 for literature, and since 1943, one for musical composition.

April 11: It was part of his war message in which he asked Congress for "forcible intervention" against Spain to establish peace in Cuba. His request was granted on April 20. The Spanish-American War, which was over a few months later, began.

April 13: President Franklin Delano Roosevelt had died on April 12. As FDR's vice-president, Truman would become President.

April 14: He said, "The South is avenged."

April 17: Possible answers are ace, age, ago, ale, arch, are, cage, cagey, cagy, car, care, cargo, cay, char, charge, chore, clay, clear, clog, cog, coo, cool, cooler, core, cry, each, ear, era, gale, galore, gay, gear, glare, glary, glory, goo, gooey, goal, gore, gory, gray, grey, hag, hale, hare, hay, heal, hear, her, hero, hoary, hog, hole, holy, lace, lacer, lacy, lag, large, lay, layer, leg, log, loge, logo, lore, lye, lyre, oar, ogre, oleo, ore, race, rag, rage, ray, reach, roe, role, yea, yeah, year, and yore. Accept other correct answers.

April 18: The San Andreas Fault is a major fracture in the Earth's crust. It results from the abutment, or touching, of two major plates of the Earth's crust. It is movement along the fault that caused the earthquake.

April 19: He said it to about 70 Minutemen during the Battle of Lexington. It began the American Revolution. "They" referred to the British.

April 20: Hot Springs National Park is in central Arkansas. It has 47 thermal springs. There are several hydrotheropeutic institutions located there. The Physical Medicine Center is also there. Over a million gallons of water with an average temperature of 143°F (62°C) flow from the spring every day.

April 23: Benjamin Franklin wrote in a 1789 letter, "...in this world nothing is certain but death and taxes."

April 24: The Library of Congress was destroyed during the War of 1812 when British troops marched on Washington, D.C., and burned the Capitol.

April 26: Audubon was an ornithologist and artist. He painted every known species of North American bird in the early 19th century. His paintings were published as *The Birds of America.* (A quatrain is a 4-lined poem.)

April 26: A clerihew is a biographical, humorous quatrain. Usually the person is named in the first line of the poem.

April 27: Facts may include some of the following: There are about 180 species. They are members of the family *Picidae* and the order *Piciformes.* They probe for insects in the tree bark. They chisel nest holes in dead wood. They occur worldwide, but they are most abundant in South America and Southeast Asia. A few temperate-zone species migrate. A few species include acorn woodpecker, great spotted woodpecker, and red-headed woodpecker.

April 28: The Monroe Doctrine warned European nations not to intervene in the Western Hemisphere.

April 29: "Onomatopoeia" is the formation or use of words that imitate what they denote. Some examples are *buzz, hiss, bang, whisper, moo, crash,* and *choochoo.*

April 30: He was engineer on the Illinois Central locomotive, Number 382. The locomotive hit the caboose of a freight train that had been incompletely switched. Jones was the only one killed. His death at the throttle of the "Cannonball" led to his rise to national fame.

May

May 2: The map should show that the U.S. gained the western half of the Mississippi River Basin in this purchase, known as the Louisiana Purchase. The size of the U.S. doubled.

May 4: He was a member of the Committee of Correspondence. This committee had been organized the previous November "for the sole purpose of corresponding with our friends in Great Britain...and other parts of the world."

May 5: Alan Shepard, Jr., was the first American astronaut to be launched into space.

May 9: White abolitionist John Brown encouraged overt action to win freedom for blacks in the U.S. In 1859 he and his small band attacked the armory at Harpers Ferry, VA. He was hanged for treason. The American Heritage Dictionary gives one definition of "martyr" as "a person who makes great sacrifices or suffers much in order to further a belief, cause, or principle."

May 10: They were called the Green Mountain Boys.

May 11: Some possible answers are as follows: aim, ant, ante, ate, east, eat, inn, main, man, mane, mat, mean, meat, men, mine, mite, moan, moat, most, name, nest, nine, not, note, oat, one, same, sane, sat, sent, sin, sit, site, smite, smote, son, stain, stead, steam, stone, tame, tan, tea, team, ten, toe, ton, and tone.

Accept other correct answers.

May 12: A limerick is a humorous, 5-lined poem. The lines are anapestic; in other words, each metrical foot is composed of 2 short syllables followed by one long one. There are 2 feet in the third and fourth lines and 3 feet in the first, second, and fifth lines.

May 13: There had been fighting with the Indians in the area. In 1614 John Rolfe married Pocahontas, the favorite daughter of Powhattan, chief of the Indians in the region. This did a great deal to bring peace to the region—at least until Powhattan died in 1618. He also helped the colony by developing a mild form of tobacco. Almost everyone started to plant it. It became so important that it was used as money. The value of things was figured in pounds of tobacco.

May 14: Some possibilities are Jello, Kleenex, Coke, Dictograph, Q-tip, and Band-Aid.

May 17: He discovered that innoculation with matter drawn from lesions of cowpox would prevent the contraction of smallpox. This discovery of vaccination greatly reduced the incidence of smallpox throughout the world.

May 20: Any man or woman 21 years of age or older could secure title to 160 acres of public land by living in it and cultivating it for 5 years and paying a fee of about $18.

May 21: The International Red Cross was established to care for victims of war. Peacetime activities include blood banks, medical clinics, and disaster relief. It provides food, clothing, shelter, and medical care after floods, earthquakes, hurricanes, fires, etc.

May 24: The message was "What hath God wrought!" In International Morse Code the message would be as follows: .--/....../.-/-/....../.-/-..//--./.--./-..//.--/.-/.---/--./....../-//

May 25: They believed people were basically good and that insight and intuition were more important than logic and experience.

May 26: She was among the first six women selected by NASA on January 16, 1978. She became the first U.S. woman to fly in space.

May 27: A suspension bridge is one having the roadway suspended from cables that are usually supported by towers. Other types of bridges are arch, beam, cantilever, ponton, and truss.

May 28: Ian Fleming's most famous character was James Bond, a high-living British secret service agent. He was also known as 007.

June

June 3: Charles Drew became an expert in the preservation and storage of human blood for later use in transfusions.

June 6: "D-Day" means an unnamed day on which an offensive is to be launched. It is especially used in reference to June 6, 1944, the day on which the Allied forces invaded France during World War II.

June 7: Dr. Waksman discovered the antibiotic streptomycin, the first specific agent effective in the treatment of tuberculosis.

June 9: Howard Carter discovered the largely intact tomb of King Tutankhamen.

June 10: She starred as Dorothy in *The Wizard of Oz*.

June 11: Kamehameha (1758-1819) was the Hawaiian conqueror and king who united all the Hawaiian islands. Known as Kamehameha the Great, he maintained Hawaii's independence throughout the difficult period of European discovery and exploration.

June 13: Ernesto Miranda's confession secured during repeated questioning helped convict him. The Supreme Court overturned the conviction with this ruling: "...The prosecution may not use statements...stemming from custodial interrogation of the defendant...unless...means are devised to inform...their right of silence..."

June 15: Ice crystals in the clouds rub against each other and become charged. If the charge is great enough, the electrons jump between the cloud and the ground or the cloud and another cloud. A huge spark, or lightning, occurs.

June 16: The nation gradually moved into a war economy.

June 18: Napoleon was defeated at the Battle of Waterloo. "Waterloo" has become synonymous with any disastrous or crushing defeat.

June 21: The sun sets for only a few minutes. At the North Pole it doesn't set at all.

June 22: It dealt with World War I.

June 24: Burr conspired with General James Wilkinson to plan an invasion of Mexico; they hoped to establish an independent government there. They also hoped to encourage parts of the West to secede and join

94

Mexico. Their goal was to found an empire with New Orleans as capital. Their plot failed before Burr had the chance to commit any overt act; therefore, he was acquitted.

June 25: Custer, a West Point graduate, commanded a Michigan cavalry brigade. He distinguished himself in many battles. At the end of the war he pursued General Lee relentlessly and contributed to Lee's eventual surrender.

June 29: The moral of the story was that the simplest things in life are best and that real wealth lies in giving to others. A sampler is a piece of cloth embroidered with various designs or mottoes.

June 30: The minimum voting age was lowered from 21 to 18.

July

July 1: It was organized by Benjamin Franklin in Philadelphia.

July 2: It was the Civil Rights Act of 1964.

July 3: Fort Necessity had been built by Major General George Washington and a body of Virginia militia. It was under Washington's control when the French and their Indian allies attacked. Major General Washington surrendered the fort to them.

July 4: The Washington Monument is an obelisk.

July 5: The Greatest Show on Earth was how he billed his circus.

July 6: It is a decoration given by the U.S.A. to civilians for outstanding services in peace or in war.

July 10: *Whistler's Mother* is the painting.

July 11: E.B. White wrote *Charlotte's Web, Stuart Little,* and *The Trumpeter Swan.*

July 13: Archaeology is the systematic retrieval and study of the material remains of humans' past. The archaeologist studies artifacts, objects produced by human workmanship. The archaeologist describes, classifies, and analyzes the artifacts.

July 14: It commemorates the capture of the Bastille, a French prison, on July 14, 1789. The prison had become a symbol of royal tyranny. Its fall was a sign that the Revolution had spread to the peasants and to the countryside.

July 16: He hit safely in 56 consecutive games, becoming the first player to get a hit in more than 50 consecutive games.

July 17: It was the first time American astronauts participated in an international spaceflight.

July 18: It was a helicopter.

July 21: Confederate forces under General Joseph Johnston defeated Union forces under General Irvin McDowell.

July 22: His plant experiments lay the foundation for the science of heredity, the passing on of genes from parents to offspring.

July 24: Under him Venezuela, Haiti, New Granada (later Colombia), Ecuador, Peru, and Upper Peru (renamed Bolivia) gained their independence from Spain.

July 25: Esperanto is an artificial universal language. Its vocabulary is based on word roots common to many European languages.

July 29: NASA stands for National Aeronautics and Space Administration.

August

Aug. 2: Hickok was a stagecoach driver, a scout for General Custer, a U.S. marshall, a sharpshooter, and a trick rider. A clerihew is a humorous quatrain about a person. That person is usually mentioned in the first line.

Aug. 4: Wallenberg is credited with personally saving between 20,000 and 100,000 Hungarian Jews from the Nazis by supplying Swedish passports for them. The only other person to receive the honor of honorary citizenship to date was Winston Churchill.

Aug. 5: It was imposed to pay Civil War expenses. It was rescinded in 1872.

Aug. 7: A eclipse is when 3 celestial bodies become aligned. In a solar eclipse the moon passes between Earth and the sun.

Aug. 8: Vice President Gerald Ford was appointed President. He then became the first President elected neither President nor vice president. (He had become vice president when Vice President Agnew resigned.)

Aug. 9: He won in track and field—100-meter run, broad jump, 200-meter run, and 400-meter relay.

Aug. 10: Mother Teresa, a Roman Catholic missionary, did much to help the starving people in the slums of Calcutta, India. In 1950 she established the Order of the Missionaries, which also included other areas

95

of the world where the need is great.

Aug. 12: She wrote the text for "America the Beautiful."

Aug. 14: They are now Hawaii.

Aug. 17: Crockett was a scout, an army officer, a congressman, and a frontiersman. He died at The Alamo.

Aug. 18: The 19th Amendment granted suffrage—the right to vote—to women.

Aug. 20: He called it a War on Poverty.

Aug. 21: Hawaii is an archipelago, or chain of islands. The Hawaiian chain includes 132 islands. The 8 main islands are Oahu, Hawaii, Maui, Kauai, Lanai, Molokai, Niihau, and Kahoolawe. The last two are not very well known. About 80% of the people live on Oahu, where the capital, Honolulu, is located. No one lives on the barren Kahoolawe.

Aug. 22: Science fiction is fiction in which actual or potential scientific discoveries and developments form part of the plot.

Aug. 25: The British had attacked the city of Washington during the War of 1812.

Aug. 26: Answers will vary, but in German *kinder* means "children" and *garten* means "garden."

Aug. 27: President John F. Kennedy had been assassinated.

Aug. 28: Charlie McCarthy was ventriloquist Edgar Bergen's dummy. It was a "degree of Master of Innuendo and Snappy Comeback." (The children might enjoy knowing that Edgar Bergen was the father of Candice Bergen, TV's "Murphy Brown.")

Aug. 29: A filibuster is the use of prolonged speechmaking in order to delay legislative action. Senator Thurmond became the first senator to filibuster for more than 24 hours. He spoke for 24 hours 18 minutes against Civil Rights legislation.

Aug. 30: Shelley is best known for *Frankenstein*. Misunderstood, the once gentle monster turns vengeful and dangerous.